THE PHILOSOPHY OF LITERARY AMATEURISM

THE
PHILOSOPHY
OF LITERARY
AMATEURISM

NAOMI LEBOWITZ

University of Missouri Press
Columbia and London

Library of Congress Cataloging-in-Publication Data

Lebowitz, Naomi.
    The philosophy of literary amateurism / Naomi Lebowitz.
        p. cm.
    Includes bibliographical references and index.
    ISBN 0-8262-0970-X
    1. Literature, Modern—History and criticism. 2. Authors and readers.
3. Amateurism. I. Title.
PN701.L43   1994
809—dc20   94-21918
                                                                   CIP

Designer: Rhonda Miller
Typesetter: Connell-Zeko Type & Graphics
Printer and binder: Thomson-Shore, Inc.
Typefaces: Lithos and New Century Schoolbook

This book is brought to publication with generous support from
Washington University, St. Louis.

to Al: master amateur

CONTENTS

ACKNOWLEDGMENTS

I would like to thank my students, especially Laura Amodie, Rori Bloom, Carl Christensen, Michael Friedman, Marian Fragola, Daniel Solove, and Terry Pruit, who helped me, with unusual intelligence and interest, to shape my subject. I am grateful to my colleagues and friends (particularly Ruth Newton and Albert Lebowitz) who read portions of this manuscript and were willing to discuss and/or live out amateurism as a philosophy in literature: Alice Bloom, Milica Banjanin, Stanley Elkin, Wayne Fields, Rockwell Gray, Pamela Hadas, Dan Kohl, Jill Levin, William Matheson, Robert and Att McDowell, John Morris, Eric Pankey, Paul Rosenzweig, Richard Ruland, Dan Shea, Benjamin Taylor, Jarvis Thurston, Mona Van Duyn, Judith Weissman, and Steven Zwicker.

I would like to thank Everyman's Library Limited for permission to reprint the essay on Italo Svevo, which was originally written as an introduction to the Everyman edition of *Confessions of Zeno,* and Duke University Press for permission to reprint a version of the essay that first appeared as "Defenses of Vengeance: Rousseau's Legacy to the Novel" in *MLQ* 46 (September 1985): 250–75.

THE
PHILOSOPHY
OF LITERARY
AMATEURISM

1

BODY, BOOK, AND CANDLE

I conceive a man's body as a kind of flame, like a candle flame, forever upright and yet flowing: and the intellect is just the light that is shed on to the things around. And I am not so much concerned with the things around—which is really mind—but with the mystery of the flame forever flowing, coming God knows how from out of practically nowhere, and being *itself*, whatever there is around it, that it lights up.

D. H. Lawrence

Why can we so confidently adopt the figure of Dostoyevsky's filial, if apocryphal, appropriation of Gogol to maintain that all professional literary writers and thinkers who are serious about amateurism as a form and philosophy have come out of Montaigne's Overcoat? Because it is an overcoat Montaigne pretends to wear reluctantly until he reminds us that the often arbitrary costume of custom, protecting against our nakedness, in fact calls attention to our "defective and indigent state," holding us to the humility of realism.[1] Virtue, like the body, is to be clothed in a topos of "no authority" to "solicit nonchalantly" both his memory and his reader (M, 1:26.109, 2:17.493). Warring against schooled philosophies and theologies in search of the naked Truth that persist in using books to cover the shame of the body, excommunicating it by ceremonies of bell, book, and candle, by systematically repressive hierarchies, Montaigne takes as his model Socrates, who "deliberately gives up his strength" to keep virtue and dialogue democratically situated at ground level (M, 1:26.120). The Périgord philoso-

---

1. Michel de Montaigne, "The Custom of Wearing Clothes," in *The Complete Essays of Montaigne,* 1:36.166; henceforth cited in the text as M, with volume, essay, and page numbers.

pher is not up to the Socratic heroism of standing barefoot on ice, wearing
the same dress in summer and winter, but that image insulates him from the
formalism that flaunts itself in a world "where fashioning and art have so
much credit and authority" (M, 3:2.611). Montaigne can surrender the ex-
trinsic mark of the schoolman, the studied pose, but he gives up, too, the
hope of living and writing naked in the "sweet freedom of nature's first laws"
(M, 3:2.611; M, "To the Reader," 2). He will constantly confess his determin-
ing conditions in order not to forget them; on the contrary, it is by a persistent tasting and pinching of his classed carelessness, his temperamental and
biological defects that abuse the classical trope of digression, his literary
paternity, his historical and domestic moment that he makes of the body of
"an admirable gossip" a moral universal of Representative Man revered by
Emerson for a "sincerity and marrow" that "reaches to his sentences."[2]

Enjoying the solitude and self-study we associate with Being, he is good
sport enough to entertain Appearance that reaches even into his den: "I
am constantly adorning myself, for I am constantly describing myself" (M,
2:6.273). He accepts the adulteration of self-knowledge by its cartooned
representation to admit the legitimacy of how he seems to those who read
and meet him in life and literature: "Painting myself for others, I have
painted my inward self with colors clearer than my original ones" (M,
2:18.504). He will not be starved or translated out of his body by severe,
unsociable, celibate predicates of purification: Essence, Reason, Miracle,
Perfection, Sin, Cure. Instead he forces *them* to give up some of their
strength, dilutes by mixed marriages essence to accident, reason to experience, miracle to nature, purity to consubstantiality, sin and cure to original
and secondary malady (M, 2:6.274, 267; 12.330; 3:13.829, 826, 835, 855).
His own just suitable marriage, made on earth, not passionate, but steady
in its mutual favor and friendship, the historical condition that houses the
casual ceremony of this surrender to sociability, serves as the great orga-
nizing metaphor of the *Essays* (M, 3:5). A domestic structure that keeps
retreats to the study merely provisional lest the priestly desire to "marry
Wisdom herself" (M, 3:5.648) freeze the hearth, thwarts glamorous temptations to climax and conversion by sponsoring a persistent and gay conversation between the body's humors and plans, postures and principles, diseases
and healths, and those of others, across categories and contradictions. The
purifying transcendental Christian communion is coaxed down to the oxy-
moron of mere experience that overcivilized philosophy calls a "barbarous
alliance": the "marriage of pleasure with necessity," "intellectually sensual,
sensually intellectual" (M, 3:13.837, 850). Of the Christian translation of

2. The epithet and comment are from "Montaigne, or the Skeptic," from *Representative Men*, in *Selected Essays of Ralph Waldo Emerson*, 321–25.

body to spirit Montaigne asks: "To what purpose . . . do we dismember by divorce a structure made up of such close and brotherly correspondence? On the contrary, let us bind it together by mutual services. Let the mind arouse and quicken the heaviness of the body, and the body check and make fast the lightness of the mind" (M, 3:13,850).

The divorce of the body from the book by which schoolmen protect the authority of their metaphysics from the humiliation of their physics (M, 3:13,821) attracts Montaigne's ferocious biologizing of all those supercelestial projections puffed forth by philosophers "perched on the epicycle of Mercury" (M, 2:17.481). The stone, the cough, the corn, the palpitation insist upon consubstantiality with philosophy, compelling it to move restlessly on the line of transition and perception between its fixed conceptual terms in the same "uncertainty, weakness, and ignorance" as its makers, so that it can become what it was meant to be, a useful consoler and confessor (M, 2:17.480). The book needs to have Montaigne's bad memory to keep the body from an education of memorized morality (M, 2:17.494). His good father was wrong to want, finally, to cure his son of his defects. If the disease that is "no less fond of life than you" is oppressed by the "tyrannical subjection" of overdoctoring instead of humored, it will return for savage revenge (M, 3:13.834–35, 837). Disease, defect, digression are the intrinsic signs that the *essais* are realizing their double-rooted entelechy, to try and to train, by keeping aesthetics and morality, epistemology and ethics as consubstantial in the amateur's book as they are in our amateur lives.[3] Catholics and Protestants are wrong to cure by civil war, theologians by unsociable miracle, philosophers by systems that want to solve by contradiction the quarrels between schemes and sclerosis, corns and conceptions. Body and spirit, unnailed from climactic crucifixions of cure, playfully and conjugally wrestle through the book, guessing at each other, like Montaigne and his ancients, like his many moods (since "there is as much difference between us and ourselves as between us and others," M, 3:13.853, 2:1.244). They stop only to eat a moveable feast at Montaigne's transitional table.

Montaigne absorbs Socrates's principle "know thyself" only because he knows the Greek philosopher by all his many postures, psychological and physical, his *bearing* toward ideas (M, 3:13.852). He appropriates the saving posture of ignorance to adulterate his formal authority as writer by his intimate and careless pleasure as reader. These passages are consubstantial: "Every day I amuse myself reading authors without any care for their learning, looking for their style, not their subject. Just as I seek the com-

---

3. See Iris Murdoch, *Metaphysics as a Guide to Morals,* 170, 177. Murdoch censures those contemporary theorists who would split the terms in the belief that "not only criticism but literature is a scientific pursuit from which value must be excluded." M, 2:18.504.

pany of some famous mind, not to have him teach me, but to come to know him. . . . I present myself standing and lying down, front and rear, on the right and left, and in all my natural postures" (M, 3:8.708, 721). The eucharistic tasting and touching of author and reader in the book is repeated for the author to reader outside the book as piecemeal, patchwork stories court each other (M, 3:2.612; 2:17.499, 1.243–44). This is the gesture most central to the anatomy of amateurism and its "gay and sociable wisdom" (M, 3:13.857). The consubstantiality in the *Essays* between the defensive mode of self-abasement (however amiably edited, in the scornful opinion of Rousseau)[4] and the offensive mode of humiliation targeting hyper-professional bookmen anxious to jump out of their skins through their books (M, 3:13.856) provokes us by a casual challenge to convert from what one disciple, William James, calls the "absolute reader" to what another, Virginia Woolf, calls active: "I love the poetic gait, by leaps and gambols. . . . It is the inattentive reader who loses my subject, not I. Some word about it will always be found off in a corner" (M, 3:9.761).[5] That reader is induced to savor, by the body's faith, the scribbled fricassee of text, and surrender, like it, some strength (M, 3:13.826). Because of this domestic arrangement, Montaigne, unlike the excommunicating egalitarian Rousseau, can transfer with aplomb rhetorical and theatrical metaphors to the task of composing character and playing the man in order to persuade to moral realism: "Our great and glorious masterpiece ["chef-d'oeuvre"] is to live appropriately" (M, 3:13.852, 851). Neither author nor reader can know or convey a naked truth by cutting a story out of whole cloth. We need to engage our dreams of perfection to guess them back to the body where they are lowered into conversation (M, 3:13.837).

Fathers, statesmen, confessors are wrong to impose cures, but "even good authors are wrong to insist on fashioning a consistent and solid fabric out of us" (M, 2:1.239). The partial stories, as William James names our inevitably rhetorical projections, of our composing self are wrestled into reality by those of our reading self.[6] Those readers we call literary philosophers, Kierkegaard, Nietzsche, William James, Santayana, have acknowledged in one way or another that they have taken into both their spirit and body "something of Montaigne's gaiety."[7] It is a deceptively "risky temper" that impels even Kierkegaard, a dialectical reader of the Absolute Idea, to give

---

4. Jean-Jacques Rousseau, *The Confessions,* 479.

5. William James, *A Pluralistic Universe,* 27; Virginia Woolf, "On Re-reading Novels," in *The Essays of Virginia Woolf,* 3:341; Virginia Woolf, "How Should One Read a Book?" in *The Common Reader,* 2:288–95.

6. William James, *Pragmatism,* 71.

7. See, for example, Richard Rorty, *Philosophy and the Mirror of Nature,* 366–67. The phrase is from Nietzsche's *Ecce Homo,* 2.3, in *Basic Writings of Nietzsche,* 699.

up some of his strength to a pseudonym whose insomniac, anxious, and acrobatic body reads Abraham's story in fear and trembling as he stutter-steps on the transition line between doubt and faith. He torments for us whole into partial stories and happy endings into misunderstanding. The dramatic bearing of the body toward the Idea reminds us that training in Christianity's realism is by posture, not principle.[8]

To the extent that all good literature is read by composers not into system and principle but out of posture in and behind the book, it carries that philosophy of amateurism which recommends, through its lover Thomas Hardy, that all readers of life and fiction be classed according to temperament.[9] Though as fearful of predilection as of theory, D. H. Lawrence reminds us how much the novel holds a mirror up to the body when he turns crucifixion to consubstantiality to keep morality consubstantial with life: "If you try to nail anything down, in the novel, either it kills the novel, or the novel gets up and walks away with the nail." That is why the novel can teach the whole man and woman, both writer and reader of reality, not "to be dead man in life": "In the novel you can see, plainly, when the man goes dead, the woman goes inert. You can develop an instinct for life, if you will, instead of a theory of right and wrong, good and bad."[10] But the fictions that can teach us best to live our amateur lives are those which seem unworried, even enthusiastic about the complicity of life with an art shamelessly entered by the writer as reader, an adulteration that invites us and characters to the kind of active consultation the newly professional Dr. Johnson endorsed, against passive patronization, as he called to his side the "common reader."[11] Against elitist, male, university readers, Virginia Woolf appropriates that associate in her essays where she pictures herself continually as an active reader whose conditioned genesis of enforced amateurism was the imprisoning and liberating library of her family in which was started the "narrative(s) of the life of an educated man's daughter . . . dependent upon father and brother in the private house of the nineteenth century."[12] Like Henry James, the reading writers of the essays walk into the novels where the ways of composing and guessing at oneself, at others, are the major moral measure. The difficulty of the task is signaled by traps and temptations to deformation, the presence of false amateurs, connoisseurs as deadly as Lord Mark and Gilbert Osmond, dilettantes as infuriating

---

8. The phrase is from D. H. Lawrence, *Phoenix: The Posthumous Papers,* 755; the pseudonym is Kierkegaard's Johannes de Silentio in *Fear and Trembling.*

9. *The Life and Work of Thomas Hardy,* 274.

10. "Why the Novel Matters," in *Phoenix,* 537–38; "Morality and the Novel," in *Phoenix,* 528, 531.

11. See discussion in Alvin Kernan, *Samuel Johnson and the Impact of Print,* chap. 6.

12. Virginia Woolf, *Three Guineas,* 37.

as Skimpole, as disappointing as Harthouse and Robert Acton. Both D. H. Lawrence and Virginia Woolf remind us often that we all start as uncritical illegitimate readers duped by wonder, and that, though gradually trained and tried, that reader should always be acknowledged in us, especially as writers of our fictions. Henry James takes up for his fellow amateurs when he protests Flaubert's hyper-professional formalism in the name of the "imperfect reader" whose "imperfect sympathies" (a virtue Woolf associates with Montaigne) resist the overtold anecdote and block the writer's overprotection and overexposure of character.[13] Madame Bovary makes a farce of the consubstantiality of book and body when neither term will surrender strength, allowing Flaubert to work his body out of his book, slip out of its alien skin (M, 1:6.274). Though a brilliant anatomist of sentimental educations, Flaubert might remind us of Balzac's spoiled poet who prefers "to be at the receiving end of impressions rather than to get into other people's skins and study the mechanism of feeling."[14]

On the other hand, Dickens enthusiastically makes himself a confederate reader to Sissy Jupe in *Hard Times,* which pictures so starkly the cost of composing the world, of closing it down, by hyper-professional patronization, as she reads "wrong" novels of fancy and myth to her father and feeds them both in a place starved out by the cartooned utilitarianism of Gradgrind that divorces representation from reality. Behind the backs of Gradgrind and Bounderby, and against their celibate "Ologies," Dickens liberates the landscape, reading by the light of philological consubstantiality, *analogy:* "Is it possible, I wonder, that there was any analogy between the case of the Coketown population and the case of the little Gradgrinds?" Consubstantial correction makes representation and reality playfully continuous, neither identical nor assimilated, though "Where the one began, and the other ended, nobody could have told with any precision." After all, claims Browning's Fra Lippo Lippi in amateur gaiety:

> we're made so that we love
> First when we see them painted, things we have passed
> Perhaps a hundred times nor cared to see;
> And so they are better, painted—better to us,
> Which is the same thing. Art was given for that;
> God uses us to help each other so,
> Lending our minds out.[15]

13. Woolf, *Essays,* 3:305, and see D. H. Lawrence's character Tom Brangwen in *The Rainbow,* chap. 1; Henry James, "Introduction to *Madame Bovary*" (1902), in *Literary Criticism,* 2:340 (*The Prefaces to the New York Edition*); Woolf, *Essays,* 2:214.

14. Honoré de Balzac, *Lost Illusions,* 412, and see letter of Gustave Flaubert to Louise Colot, April 6, 1953, in *Selected Letters of Gustave Flaubert,* 151.

15. *Hard Times,* 99, 225, 67, 72; "Fra Lippo Lippi," lines 300–306.

In the name of a wise and wide reality, Dickens wields the satiric pen for his tellers of partial stories, for their open meeting of mystery, wonder, and muddle, spearing by abbreviation the calculating and absolutist cartooners of reality with epithets that avenge us for allegories; the "Bully of Humility," threatened by the partial stories of others, is punished for his boast about the "Hands": "I can read 'em off like a book." All the depth exiled by the fabricated whole stories of calculating and self-protecting dilettantes and hyper-professionals prowls around the cage of Coketown. Harthouse's confession does not correct him as reader: "I'm not a moral sort of fellow." On the contrary, it abbreviates Louisa as much as her father's reading: "to be sure, the better and profounder part of her character was not within his scope of perception; for in natures, as in seas, depth answers unto depth." Even the pain that is such an intimate companion to Montaigne is forced to wander orphaned from the indolent and torpid bodies draped on indifferent furniture: "'I think there's a pain somewhere in the room,' said Mrs. Gradgrind, 'but I couldn't positively say that I have got it.'" And Louisa's intensity of interest, which William James links to the moral life, continually blocked, is "an interest gone astray like a banished creature . . . hiding in solitary places." Her body, bullied by the book, is made sterile and sexless by the caricatures who spy to keep from seeing, making consubstantial only selfishness and a weak self. The brutal abortion of Fact is countered by the long, patient, winding line of love (a bearing toward an idea), Sleary's account of "the wayth of the dogth" who, in the *human* interest, gossip their way home.[16]

The rich, imperfect elaboration of the local calling unto the depth of spirit is named, by Ruskin, Gothic *humility,* a term that (just before they are estranged by modernity) makes aesthetic posture and moral motive consubstantial.[17] This humility, manifested in the Browning whom Ruskin admired, the lusty lover of an age of transition that tormented its prophets, lights up the face of Fra Lippo Lippi entering his own painting and duped into awe by the company of spiritual figures he himself had painted. Hardy, in touch with Ruskin's definition, and dedicated to the amateur "mode of regard," complained that Matthew Arnold's desire to live in the idea ambitiously gobbles up provincial curiosities enthusiastically enjoyed by the Wessex writer helping the local to gossip its way toward revelation.[18] The humility that Ruskin sees in the most living architecture is to the writer as

16. *Hard Times,* 108, 254, 196, 224, 98, 308.

17. "The Nature of Gothic," in *The Stones of Venice* (New York: Peter Fenelon Collier and Son, 1900), 206–7 (#78).

18. Phrase of Hardy in *Life and Work of Thomas Hardy,* 235. See *Life,* 151, and Matthew Arnold, "The Function of Criticism in the Present Time," in *Complete Prose Works,* 3:267. Woolf in *Essays,* 2:161, writes of our interest in the private lives of writers: "even their old shoes have a way of being worn on this side rather than on that, which seems not gossip but revelation."

reader a bearing toward the Idea by the most living literature in constant transition. But the ambitions of readers in the academies, to suppress the local by a synthetic global style, to cure by political in-house contradiction, to possess by the reduction of representative play and moral argument to sociological pathology and irresponsible wonder (with a concomitant diffusion of plot), ironically, crucify professions and professionals against each other. Disciplines are forced to be more and more celibate or parasitic, competitive and tyrannical, ashamed of communing and composing out of their natural and local conditionings of defect, design, disease. Our literary critics may parade their own representative pathologies, but only to belittle by political formulas those of their subjects, not to put them into conversation. When they link professional codification of social institutions and arguments, even those dedicated to the health of the humanities, intent on promoting their power, to the desire to cure by war, Virginia Woolf and Italo Svevo speak for the amateur we so desperately need now, willing to turn conditions into agents of life against false moralities and the politics of the literal. Could hyper-professionals, like "the daughters of educated men," the amateur family speculator, give up some of their strength to guess at and by imperfect sympathies, they could break themselves out into a world of gay sociable wisdom. In *To the Lighthouse,* Woolf forces competitive academic discourse and ambition to flounder on holiday where the marginal minds of women as mother and artist neutralize condescension. Any potential condescension of art to marriage is leveled by Lily's awkward compliment, in the spirit of Mrs. Ramsay, to a chastened Mr. Ramsay, before she is able to finish her painting. And Woolf turns us to new ways of reading lives, the lives of professional women, to teach us to make of our angry sexual, political, psychological beginnings the temperamental premise of an amateurism that could keep even fanatical feminism from obliterating the memory of the view from the margins.[19] This is the saving scandal and stumbling block in the path of her own fiction's high professional attraction to the dissolution of moral argument in aesthetic musing. Montaigne's descendants, William and Henry James, Joseph Conrad, Honoré de Balzac, George Santayana, Italo Svevo, Robert Frost, Wallace Stevens, subjects of the following essays, have this in common: by their constant attention to the moral and aesthetic imperative of reading our bodies, with theirs, into their books, they help us to see and to sense well and justly the deepest and widest life available to us in a cosmos liberated into consubstantiality with our literatures.

19. *Three Guineas,* esp. 17, 39, 66, 106–11, 124–25, 130. See the ending of Italo Svevo, *Confessions of Zeno.* Of parallel, if not specific, interest to this focus on the legacy of Montaigne is that of Judith Shklar, *Ordinary Vices.*

2

TEMPERAMENT WITH A TONGUE

The American Education of the Possible Poet
by the Possible Philosopher—William James,
George Santayana, Wallace Stevens, and Robert Frost

> The lords of life, the lords of life,
> I saw them pass,
> In their own guise,
> Like and unlike,
> Portly and grim,
> Use and Surprise,
> Surface and Dream,
> Succession swift and spectral Wrong,
> Temperament without a tongue . . .
> Emerson, "Experience"

I am an ignorant man, almost a poet . . .

George Santayana

I. Introduction

The long-acknowledged intellectual relations between the philosophies
of William James and Santayana and the poetry of Stevens and Frost have
been largely explored in their linguistic, ontological, epistemological, political, and sexual implications. We have been made to feel how the patterns
of pragmatism have both ethical and aesthetic consequences for our read-

ing.[1] What has not been emphasized, however, is the dramatic sociability, often cast as marginal anecdote, emanating from the philosophers' political cartooning of the temperaments, rather than principles, of philosophies and philosophers past and present, including themselves and each other. It is a central paradigm and agency for the making of healthy and full psychological and moral perspectives, this poetry of continual conversation with the moody universe. The philosophical and poetic strategy of characterizing competing tempers resists the persistent intellectual temptation to suppress, by recourse to fixed systems of thought, personal preference and motive. In the name of a richer reality, curtailed and constricted by deforming idealisms, the gossip of temperament is enlisted to liberate, in our relations with the natural as well as the intellectual world, an authentic, responsive, creative moral and spiritual dimension and energy. The American philosophers influenced the American poets in the manner of Eliot's Montaigne, who infects us before we can criticize him, and this sense of incarnate learning by contagion is reflected in the following pages.

II. Gossip and Spirit

In a letter of 1943, Stevens, commenting on "Notes toward a Supreme Fiction," takes us back to his days at Harvard when, as a student, along with Frost, of Santayana and William James, he learned it might "be possible to yield, or to try to yield" to a "declared fiction." In his wide thinking for the collective mind he suggests: "This is the same thing as saying that it might be possible for us to believe in something that we know to be untrue. Of course, we do that every day, but we don't make the most of the fact that we do it out of the need to believe, what in your day, and mine, in Cambridge was called the will to believe."[2]

The need to believe binds, as a phrase, the poverty of our temperamental fate with the imaginative necessity to consult spirit and, by doing so, releases the first from its theological humiliation and the second from its theological inflation. Of all the pragmatist revisions of sterile and system-

1. The most recent and interesting of these explorations, for my emphasis, is Richard Poirier's *Poetry and Pragmatism,* which develops out of Emerson a generous tradition of "linguistic skepticism" that helps to renew the world as we read it. See also his *Robert Frost: The Work of Knowing,* for his discussion of the performing stance, and *The Renewal of Literature: Emersonian Reflections.* Other recent comparable treatments of interest include those of Ross Posnock, *The Trial of Curiosity: Henry James, William James, and the Challenge of Modernity;* Frank Lentricchia, *Ariel and the Police: Michel Foucault, William James, Wallace Stevens;* and Margaret Peterson, *Wallace Stevens and the Idealist Tradition.* See also Frank Lentricchia, *Robert Frost: Modern Poetics and the Landscape of Self.*
2. Wallace Stevens, *Letters of Wallace Stevens,* 443; henceforth cited in the text as WS, *Ltrs.*

atic hierarchies in philosophy, this was the most essential and exciting, and it was accomplished by making facts and terms psychical. Santayana approves of Bertrand Russell's reminder that "where others might think of the starry heavens, pragmatists think of the perception of the starry heavens; where others think of God, pragmatists think of the belief in God, and so on."[3] Here is the shift that engendered in Frost the boldness to make us attend to the gravity behind his parody of Corinthian virtues: "I venture to say that the greatest of the three is Gossip. It may be defined as our guessing at each other. . . . Gossip exalts in poetry. Poetry is the top of our guessing at each other. The beauty of gossip is that it is the whole of our daily life. It has flashes of insight. The height of imagination is there."[4] The apparent deflation of poetry's place to the context of the novel's gossip,[5] which guesses at the inner seriousness of hints, double entendres, "sound-postures," displacements, inferences, wit around trees, across work, behind doors, in the "dramatic tones of voice" of neighbors engaged in "talking by contraries," is a move to preserve the romance of temperament against its identity as fate, so it can serve, not block, the mystery of spirit.[6]

Spirit, joined to gossip by a shared dimension, "the height of imagination," is made by William James and Santayana to play at the level of poetry where their American poets guess at the "possible nest in the invisible tree" and taste "at the root of the tongue the unreal of what is real."[7] It is asked to be unashamed of its origins in animal faith, its cravings and needs, of its reliance on "partial purposes" and "partial stories" by which we forage in the motley universe, content not to master it.[8] When spirit enjoys the moody gossip of temperament with a tongue, too long silenced in the name of human pride or prejudice by monisms and idealisms, materialisms and positivisms, it doubles the dimension of a world divided by dualism's "lordship over the whole of life."[9] When we admit that "absolute truth . . . scorns to be known," we know what our task is as possible philosophers: "The function of mind is rather to increase the wealth of the universe in the spiritual dimension, by adding appearance to substance and passion to

3. George Santayana, *Winds of Doctrine,* 125; henceforth cited in the text as GS, *Winds.*
4. Robert Frost, *Robert Frost: Poetry and Prose,* 351; henceforth cited in the text as RF, *P&P.* Stanley Burnshaw, *Robert Frost Himself,* 253.
5. See Patricia Meyer Spacks, *Gossip.*
6. Robert Frost, "Robert Frost: The Art of Poetry, II," 113; henceforth cited in the text as RF, "Art." Robert Frost, *Robert Frost on Writing,* 153, 282; henceforth cited in the text as RF, *Writing.*
7. Wallace Stevens, *The Collected Poems,* 437, 313; henceforth cited in the text as WS, *Poems.*
8. William James, *Pragmatism,* 71; henceforth cited in the text as WJ, *Prag.* William James, *Some Problems of Philosophy,* 69; henceforth cited in the text as WJ, *Phil.*
9. William James, *A Pluralistic Universe,* 109; henceforth cited in the text as WJ, *Plur.*

necessity, and by creating all those private perspectives, and those emotions of wonder, adventure, curiosity, and laughter which omniscience would exclude."[10]

Temperament, released from its long house arrest as Fate (by hierarchies of Beyonds and Belows in "tenements of rose and ice," WS, *Poems,* 239), fairly leaps into the guessing game sponsored by pragmatic philosophies that boldly claim: "our worst difficulties arise from the assumption that knowledge of existences ought to be literal, whereas knowledge of existences has no need, no propensity, and no fitness to be literal" (GS, *Phil,* 399). This reminder seems a rebuke to our contemporary academies, which depersonalize tone and confine referentiality to political categories in order to deny literature its full and Platonically dangerous representative power. Systematic philosophies and theologies, "too exactly" themselves (WS, *Poems,* 310), too "through and through" (WJ, *Prag,* xii), cannot keep the many moods of temperament from costuming the facts of our instrumental life and from depicting that life on a stage "in a sense more truly than [in] history" (GS, *Phil,* 400). It is not stagestruck temperament but its compulsive degradation by totalitarian philosophies that "puts all divinity to rout,"[11] turning essence and spirit into enemies of a life rich in appearances. The new American context rests on the promotion to active ethical power of primordial perception, an exuberant and humble impresario of "actual seemings" (WS, *Poems,* 340). Like all pragmatists of perception, Santayana insists on putting himself smack into the middle of the play to rehearse the discriminations that constitute the life, not the logic, of Reason: "the images of sense and science will not delude me if instead of hypostatising them, I regard them as graphic symbols for home and for the way there. That such external things exist, that I exist myself, and live more or less prosperously in the midst of them, is a faith not founded on reason but precipitated in action, and in that intent, which is virtual action, involved in perception" (GS, *Phil,* 403).

The constant greetings and jibes to offstage spirit, "addressed and consulted and required in everything that the theatre contrives" (GS, *Phil,* 447) by onstage temperament, give voice to the "planetary pass-pass" (WS, *Poems,* 425) of a cosmos we know only as "the workshop of being, where we catch fact in the making" of our necessary fictions (WJ, *Prag,* 138). The banishing of absolutism and omniscience from this "moonlit and dream visited planet"[12] recovers for us, willing to be "authors of novelty"

10. George Santayana, *The Philosophy of Santayana,* 478; henceforth cited in the text as GS, *Phil.*
11. Ralph Waldo Emerson, *Selections from Ralph Waldo Emerson,* 258; henceforth cited in the text as Em.
12. William James, *The Will to Believe,* 22; henceforth cited in the text as WJ, *Will.*

(WJ, *Phil,* 75), "insatiable actors" (WS, *Poems,* 240), all that has been banished by "the great de-realizer of the only life we are at home in" and, thereby, "redeems the nature of reality from essential foreignness" (WJ, *Plur,* 28). Temperament exorcises the pejorative bias that has crippled it and fixed it as the curse that even "penetrates the ameliorations of education and experience of life."[13] It becomes a positive player in Santayana's theater of meditation and sensation where reading understudies acting so that writing can become, not mere spectatorship, but deed. Emerson pits the deed of "Man Thinking" in the universe against the deadness of the bookworm protected against its otherness (Em, 67); *his* reader, William James, keeps, in the manner of Montaigne, our bodies consubstantial with our books: "The books of all the great philosophers are like so many men. Our sense of an essential personal flavor in each one of them, is the finest fruit of our accomplished philosophic education. What the system pretends to be is a picture of the great universe of God. What it is—and so flagrantly—is the revelation of how intensely odd the personal flavor of some fellow creature is" (WJ, *Prag,* 24). Temperament takes back the authority of revelation that condemned it and activates spirit by reading the universe through the distorting glass of psychology and interested perception "held against the world of hoary grass."[14] William James romances the fate out of facts, "squirming" and fringed with feeling (WS, *Poems,* 215), and into action by "a stroke of intuitive sympathy with the thing" (WJ, *Plur,* 117).

The transfer to this literary conceit of an authority formerly reserved for the Truth, supreme and uncostumed, to regain in our descriptions a genuine sense of the universe, eases all the *unnecessary* resistance, discord, dualism we moderns have taken for granted. More crucial, even, than collapsing the pretentious disjunction between logic and psychology[15] is negotiating the one between psychology and spirit:

> Psychology and religion . . . both admit that there are forces seemingly outside of the conscious individual that bring redemption to his life. Nevertheless, psychology, defining these forces as "subconscious," and speaking of their effects as due to "incubation," or "cerebration," implies that they do not transcend the individual's personality; and herein she diverges from Christian theology, which insists that they are direct supernatural operations of the Deity. I propose to you that we do not yet consider this divergence final, but leave the

13. Wallace Stevens, *The Necessary Angel: Essays on Reality and the Imagination,* 120; henceforth cited in the text as WS, *Essays.*
14. Robert Frost, *The Poetry of Robert Frost: Collected Poems,* 68; henceforth cited in the text as RF, *Poems.*
15. William James, *The Meaning of Truth,* 252.

question . . . in abeyance—continued inquiry may enable us to get rid of some of the apparent discord.[16]

By shamelessly grounding religion in varieties of temperamental experience, James undercuts Freud as enemy of Christianity, coaxing psychology and spirit to guess at each other in temperament's theater, to speak the language of "literary psychology," which yields us, by "the art of imagining how [animals] feel and think" the most "adequate sort of knowledge of which a mind is capable" (GS, *Phil,* 434, 421). In this way, we are asked to adulterate all the tales of absolute readers ambitious to get beyond their fictions. As temperamentalists, we are, writes James "the very personages of the world-drama. In your own eyes each of you here is its hero, and the villains are your respective friends or enemies. The tale which the absolute reader finds so perfect, we spoil for one another through our several vital identifications with the destinies of the particular personages involved." The sympathetic or competitive "divining of someone else's inner life" in the name of restoring full thickness to the universe stays on the level at which we speak our lines, in a welter of partial stories, the level from which we launch our active and adequate morality (WJ, *Plur,* 27–28).

While Schopenhauer, compelled by what Nietzsche calls the temper of "the tortured man seeking release from his torment,"[17] locates, to shame our willful and restless discords, the origin of philosophizing in the imagination of extinction, of a universe happy to be rid of its human parasites, James characteristically contends it should derive from the imagination of a primordial instinct of interested guessing at each other. He warms Emerson's Rock as he passes it on to Stevens, the Rock we cover with the "queer assertion of humanity" (WS, *Poems,* 525) and its fictions:

> were all other things, gods and men and starry heavens, blotted out from this universe, and were there left but one rock with two loving souls upon it, that rock would have as thoroughly moral a constitution as any possible world which the eternities and immensities could harbor. It would be a tragic constitution, because the rock's inhabitants would die. But while they lived, there would be real good things and real bad things in the universe; there would be obligations, claims, and expectations; obediences, refusals, and disappointments; compunctions and longings for harmony to come again, and inward peace of conscience when it was restored; there would in short, be a moral life, whose active energy would have no limit but the intensity of interest in each other with which the hero and heroine might be endowed. (WJ, *Will,* 197)

16. William James, *The Varieties of Religious Experience,* 211; henceforth cited in the text as WJ, *Var.*
17. Friedrich Nietzsche, *The Genealogy of Morals,* 240.

To understand in the fashion, as Royce's Bergson puts it, "in which one loves" and longs keeps our philosophies mindful of their genesis in the "clash of human temperaments" that spawned them and our poetry from escaping moral responsibility by arresting us in old nostalgias and pathetic fallacies (WJ, *Plur,* 119; *Prag,* 11). The "latest freed" tempers of American philosophy, "Escaped from the truth" (WS, *Poems,* 204), gossip into life the poetry they educated. They gave Frost, in deprecating his own aesthetic motives, the boldness to mock the authority of the Romantic sublime that would inflate the "thrill of sincerity" in the elemental "speaking voice" of neighbors: "I made the discovery in doing the Death of the Hired Man that I was interested in neighbors for more than merely their tones of speech— and always had been. I remember about when I began to suspect myself of liking their gossip for its own sake."[18] The honoring of the body's gossip for its "intimacy" and "actuality" can undo both the Romantic and Freudian sublimation that had weakened the invigorating moral animus between humors and faiths: "The ruling passion in man is not as Viennese as is claimed. It is rather a gregarious instinct to keep together by minding each other's business. Grex rather than sex" (RF, *Ltrs,* 159; *P&P,* 401). The mischievous digging up of the "cemetery of nobilities" where we raise monuments to bodies in which we have not lived reverses the reduction of the world's romance to the family romance and the romance of sacrifice, the "Dominion of the blood and sepulchre" (WS, *Essays,* 35; *Poems,* 67). Freed from fixed definition into the "radiant and productive atmosphere" of doubled dimension, nobility spreads out over the field of the visible and invisible as it "resolves itself into an enormous number of vibrations, movements, changes" (WS, *Essays,* 62, 34). And it is spoken by poetry's gossip, which obsessively joins the perceived and the possible in a diction that guesses out the "whole of our daily life."[19]

To keep Dr. Johnson from becoming a monument of nobility, Boswell read him by his body's frailties, tempers, humors.[20] Since that body is "the palmary instance of the ambiguous," it keeps dramatic conflicts, the "many curious personal ways of falling short," from the cure of contradiction courted by systematic philosophies.[21] By this kind of secular *kenosis,* the American poet, like Montaigne, "seems to confer his identity on the reader" and, at the same time, insists that "the earth is not a building but a body."[22] In this

18. Robert Frost, *Selected Letters of Robert Frost,* 159; henceforth cited in the text as RF, *Ltrs.*

19. Burnshaw, *Frost Himself,* 253.

20. Spacks, *Gossip,* 101.

21. William James, *Essays in Radical Empiricism,* 69, 45; henceforth cited in the text as WJ, *Essays;* WJ, *Prag,* 25.

22. Wallace Stevens, *Opus Posthumous: Poems, Plays, Prose,* 185–86; henceforth cited in the text as WS, *Opus.*

role, he becomes "the intermediary between people and the world in which they live and, also, between people as between themselves; but not between people and some other world" when that other world is the refuge of an absolute Beyond (WS, *Opus,* 189). Santayana teaches the poets to exchange the standard "claim to inspiration" for the cravings of animal *animus,* both inspiriting and cranky, a willing demotion warmly embraced by Frost (RF, *P&P,* 358). That poet's aging Browning "lost his moods somewhere" and became, alas, a "master" (RF, *Writing,* 157). And what a consolation to receive the philosopher's promise that by such a surrender of dignity we might "almost . . . pierce the illusions of . . . animal dogmatisms" and, in some sense, "transcend the relativity of . . . knowledge and the flightiness of . . . passions by acknowledging them with good grace" (GS, *Phil,* 479). It is a thick world of gossip we enter, of "continual conversation" with the earth, with our "many selves," as "heroes and heroines" when we renounce the bodiless beyonds and sublimes of dualistic philosophies and overinspired poetries that kept our "mid-day air" from "swarming / With the metaphysical changes that occur, / Merely in living as and where we live" (WS, *Poems,* 359, 326). James prepares the ground for these lines and the branches for many of the mock nests of Stevens's syllogisms by his imperative reminder: "But if, as metaphysicians, we are more curious about the inner nature of reality or about what really makes it go, we must turn our backs upon our winged concepts altogether, and bury ourselves in the thickness of those passing moments over the surface of which they fly, and on particular points of which they occasionally rest and perch" (WJ, *Plur,* 112).

The wonder to which we are returned by new readings from the thick of things, in Santayana's crucial conceit, "seize[s] a fact by its skirts from some unexpected quarter, and give[s] it a nickname which it might be surprised to hear, such as the rainbow or the Great Bear." The "rapid, pregnant, often humorous" names we assign to "things and for their odd ways of behaving are like those which country people give to flowers"; because they are *virtually* active and instrumental, they guide the most essential readings we can make: "they often pointedly describe how things look or what they do to us. The ideas we have of things are not fair portraits; they are political caricatures made in the human interest; but in their partial way they may be masterpieces of characterization and insight" (GS, *Phil,* 401; cf. WJ, *Prag,* 121–22).

This assumption of the way we should read the world and the philosophers and poets who act in it is crucial for the pragmatists who revel in anecdotes and asides, caricatures and partial stories "made in the human interest" to keep us moral citizens of the Rock. Santayana sets this caricaturing *against* conceptual abbreviation and makes its acknowledged marginality and partiality the legitimization of its authority to transpose our readings from the essentialist mode into the instrumental; by this move, the healthy energies of any given temperament, so long shamed by determinisms, monisms, idealisms, mysticisms, medical materialisms, are freed to active moral testing. From this posture, "insatiable actors" make out of their temperamental poetry "canon central in itself / The thesis of the plentifullest John" (WS, *Poems,* 240, 345). They engender for us the imagination of centrality by keeping their feet moving toward it. Stevens ruefully and longingly mocks essentialist thinking by his conditionals and capitals:

> It would be enough
> If we were ever, just once, at the middle, fixed
> In This Beautiful World of Ours and not as now,
> Helplessly at the edge . . .
>
> (WS, *Poems,* 430)

As a young reader, Wordsworth fed and dreamed upon a central canon that would make of his body a "poor earthly casket of immortal verse,"[23] but for these new readers, their own books are insatiable theaters through which they act (WS, *Opus,* 184).

Reading each other and ourselves gaily by animating caricatures, asides, anecdotes, epithets is a central *ethical* activity of the discriminating life of reason, as Santayana defines it. As much as that of Socrates, the life of reason knows its partial perspective is the beginning of wisdom because it exposes the absolutist cheat that evades the anxieties of marginalism. The vigorous self-irony in the self-aggrandizement of "A Rabbit as King of the Ghosts" (WS, *Poems,* 209) is precisely what punctures monistic bloat. When we hear epithets circling around the head of Santayana, "pessimistic Platonist," "harmonious skeptic," "inquisitor of structures";[24] around that of James, "a mystic in love with life," "the dupe of his desire";[25] hear Stevens entitle himself "spiritual epicure" (WS, *Ltrs,* 394) and a "Man Whose Pharynx Was Bad" (WS, *Ltrs,* 394; *Poems,* 96); or Frost term his temper one of "engaging cowardice" (RF, *P&P,* 299)—a stance that suggests the double design of defense and offense in the drama of guessing at ourselves and each other—we are not standing in the wings of their vision, but center stage. This is the place from which we can ingeniously get "into danger legitimately" in order to be "genuinely rescued" and keep, in the midst of talking contraries, our competitors "in play," but "far out of gunshot" (RF, *Writing,* 76; *P&P,* 299). The cunning insight into each ontogenetic tempera-

23. William Wordsworth, *The Prelude* (1850), 5.1.164.

24. William James, *The Selected Letters of William James,* 182; henceforth, cited in the text as WJ, *Ltrs.* WS, *Poems,* 122, 510.

25. George Santayana, *Character and Opinion in the United States,* 88; henceforth cited in the text as GS, *Char.*

ment, the "stresses [it] invites" and those it "avoids," the light in which it basks, from which it "shrinks" (WS, *Essays,* 122), begins the moral education of our phylogenetic temperament, the education that helps us to discriminate, both now and in the past, healthy from unhealthy fictions for belief. Political caricatures and the nicknames we give philosophic perspectives and tempers, the "revelation of how intensely odd the personal flavor of some fellow creature is" as he invents his noblest visions, are the live hypotheses by which James moves us, in Emerson's wake, to the virtual action of prospective moral possibilities and promises (WJ, *Prag,* 24; Em, 51). They become the comedians, canons, presidents, princes of peacocks and of proverbs of poverty, bantams, berserks, Phosphors, Ariels, Hoons, high-toned Christian, ordinary, and so-and-so women, philosophers, painters, musicians real and fictive, census takers and star splitters, minor and oven birds, old men and servants to servants, menders of walls and tramps.

III. A Conversation: Santayana and William James

A famous anecdote, confirmed in a letter by Santayana, has the philosopher crossing the street to William James, just after the publication of *The Varieties of Religious Experience:* "You have done the religious slumming of all time," he quips; to which James is said to have hummed: "Santayana's marble mind."[26] We can imagine that the motives are something more, here, than the "love of personal conquest over the philosopher across the way" (WJ, *Will,* 77), though that response counts in the exchange. Santayana is energizing the life of Reason with temperament. This "slumming" spawned, to the same purpose, Frost's favorite and familiar crossing with Stevens: "The trouble with you, Robert, is that you write about subjects; the trouble with you, Wallace, is that you write *bric a brac*";[27] the exchange is capped by Stevens in his inscription to a book of his poetry sent to Frost: "S'more bric a brac" (RF, "Art," 99). What is involved is an investment in reading and caricaturing as virtual action, not just in and around the books, but as "canon central." The philosophers' titles and caricatures of styles slum in an avid adoption of *amateurism.* They ask: "Is Life Worth Living," speak of "The Sentiment of Rationality," "Interpretations of Poetry and Religion," "Character and Opinion," "Winds of Doctrine," "Obiter Scripta," "Dialogues in Limbo," the poetry of barbarism. The essays finger the prejudices of the genteel tradition, of democratic populism, rejoice over

26. Gerald E. Myers, *William James: His Life and Thought,* 462. The robust jocularity of this American cartooning contrasts with the Pierrot pathos of Laforgue and Corbière taken into American poetry by Eliot and Pound. See also George Santayana, "Apologia Pro Mente Sua," 499.

27. Burnshaw, *Frost Himself,* 57.

the anti-intellectualism of Bergson, regret the absence of that philosopher's craving for the "merely ideal," condemn Spencer for "the hurdy-gurdy monotony" of his "dry schoolmaster temperament" and rescue him because "we feel his heart to be *in the right place* philosophically," slam Browning for "the perpetual vagrancy" of his poetic temperament's barbarism and discover a respect for the experiential base of Emerson as a "Puritan mystic with a poetic fancy."[28] Can we doubt the American origin of the chosen amateurism, the marginal and "Downward comparisons" (RF, *Poems,* 279) in the poets of asides and anecdotes, apostrophic teases, colloquies and gubbinals, variations and cadenzas, bagatelles and extracts, talking contraries, patronizations and counter-patronizations, the minor songs of much diminished things (RF, *Poems,* 119), of all the "somethings" that signal the "oblique power" generated out of the incessant "luminous flitterings" between the margins we live in and the centers we imagine from them (Em, 257; WS, *Poems,* 396)?

The illustrative airing between Santayana and William James of moody animus in the human interest promotes in the citizens of the Rock a natural moral life resistant to professional prescriptions and principles that, trying to cure our humors, have only alienated us from them. It is by his half-patronizing political caricature of William James, the competitor, that Santayana's romantic courtship of Catholic and Platonic mythology as a haven for his celibate temper of high aestheticism and skepticism is submerged in the distracting atmosphere of democratic collisions. William James's undiscriminating evangelical and democratic protestantism, of both cultural and personal origins, reconciles him to the quirky company of "miracle-workers," as does "his great charity," part of his "hunter's instinct to follow a scent" (GS, *Char,* 52). The same traits put him in the middle of philosophy as in "a maze in which he happened to find himself wandering" and looking for a way out. He lived all his life as a child with grown-ups who used philosophy as a hiding place, a "consolation and sanctuary," turning it into one of life's "natural enemies" (GS, *Char,* 57). The mixture of envy, admiration, disdain, and comparison that marks Santayana's assessments of the James who must be both protected and taunted is returned: "The great event in my life recently has been the reading of Santayana's book. Although I absolutely reject the platonism of it, I have literally squealed with delight at the imperturbable perfection with which the position is laid down on page after page." To understand a philosophic perspective well enough to characterize it as his "pessimistic platonism" or "my crass pluralism," implies James, is to realize that these views are "so many reli-

28. WJ, *Plur* 101, 122; WJ, *Prag,* 26; GS, *Winds,* 66. George Santayana, *Interpretations of Poetry and Religion,* 125, 138; henceforth cited in the text as GS, *Interp.*

gions, ways of fronting life," that give energy even to "a representative of moribund Latinity" to "rise up and administer . . . reproof to us barbarians in the hour of our triumph." The sight of a temperament exploding into faith excites James, but, including himself in the company of Santayana's barbarians, Whitman and Browning, he deflects Santayana's attack: "there is something profoundly alienating in his unsympathetic tone, his 'preciousness' and superciliousness. . . . The same things in Emerson's mouth would sound entirely different. E. receptive, expansive, as if handling life through a wide funnel with a great indraught; S. as if through a pin-point orifice that emits his cooling spray outward over the universe like a nose-disinfectant from an 'atomizer'" (WJ, Ltrs, 182–84).

The delighted imaginative sympathy at a stroke is countered by the defensive discrimination that prevents the assimilation Santayana, himself, identifies as the disease of mysticism, "a recurrent manifestation of lost equilibrium and interrupted growth."[29] In the absence of comparative cartooning, the philosophic complaints of philosophers sound to James like the "sick shriekings of . . . dying rats" lacking "the purgatorial note" (WJ, Var, 38). Stevens is almost seduced into this evasion when he notes his attraction to Santayana's resignation: "I have always, somewhat sadly, bowed to expediency or fate" (WS, Ltrs, 635). But like his philosopher, he turns from the seductive surrender back into bold battles of blooded animal faith and soars into the mock ascent of imagination's virtual action, a gesture behind which Helen Vendler persuasively hears the squeamish and ascetic desperation of Platonic longing.[30]

When Santayana implies that Bergson is an unacknowledged mystic (GS, Winds, 88), he is really acknowledging his own illegitimate attraction to floating in spirit's perfect skepticism above the anxieties of psyche and the urgency of the animal faith that spawned it.[31] The peace and play of this position constantly tempt him, chaste with longing, to "maintain himself acrobatically at that altitude," but irony comes to the rescue to show him that he is impossibly confined even "in a very sweet and marvelous solitude," where everything has lost its "urgency" and "venom" (GS, Phil, 405, 395, 397; WS, Poems, 437). It is precisely the "discussion" excited by temperamental jousting and flyting that "forces [him] to break away from a complete skepticism" that might shield him: "Instead, I have frankly

29. George Santayana, Reason in Religion, 278; henceforth cited in the text as GS, Rel.
30. Words Chosen Out of Desire, 22–26. The discussion of "self-contempt" in "The Motive for Metaphor" as a symptom of the pain of "sacrificing" the "absolutist Platonic self" is particularly persuasive, as is her constant emphasis on Stevens as a poet of mood. It is interesting to see how Stevens displaced onto Nature the "cripple" metaphor James attached to men (WJ, Plur, 158–59).
31. Santayana, "Apologia Pro Mente Sua," 532–33; GS, Phil, 405.

taken nature by the hand, accepting as a rule in my farthest speculations the animal faith I live by from day to day" (GS, *Phil,* 450). Lodged in the body, spirit needs to suffer the sense of disappointment impelled by descents into satire. If the "disintoxication" from successive illusions accomplished, provisionally, by spirit would not be habitually adulterated, it could easily lead the Santayana who chose a convent in Rome for the last days of his body to "blow out the candle, and to bed" (GS, *Phil,* 413, 418–19; *Winds,* 248). That flickering candle, sometimes small, sometimes high, that finds its way into so many of Stevens's poems, including his homage to Santayana in Rome, is set against the sun of life's noon, the dark of life's night, as the necessary light of dramatic imagination by which spirit reads, distinguishing only rich from poor illusion. And the philosopher confesses: "so long as I remain awake and the light burning, . . . total dogmatic skepticism is . . . an impossible attitude" (GS, *Phil,* 419).

Santayana's temptation to a "perpetual celibacy" and "chastity of the intellect" must necessarily engage itself in political caricaturing, slumming, guessing, gossip, so that the philosopher's temperament could learn to recognize and acknowledge its fear of being taken in by passionate prejudice (GS, *Phil,* 390). He can spend his holidays in spirit, but like his poet, to whom he gave, with James, the image, he must finally enjoy them in reality (GS, *Phil,* 391, 475). James can also *imagine* moral holidays from "the strenuous mood" in Hegelian speculation, but it is his *example* that helps Santayana, his student and colleague, resist his temper's fear of becoming a dupe (WJ, *Plur,* 57; *Prag,* 290). For James, "Philosophy was not . . . what it has been to so many, a consolation and sanctuary in a life which would have been unsatisfying without it" (GS, *Char,* 57); like existences itself, it undergoes "perpetual re-birth" (GS, *Phil,* 15). He could give to Santayana's less "gullible nature" more courage to "entertain . . . illusion without succumbing to it" by accepting as the most fundamental of givens that "temperaments with their cravings and refusals do determine men in their philosophies, and always will" (GS, *Char,* 54–55, 57–58; WJ, *Prag,* 24; GS, *Phil,* 393); and he could inspire Stevens to recover the imagination that "we spurned and crave" (WS, *Poems,* 88).

Forced to read each other with the "courage to be an amateur" (WS, *Opus,* 195), Santayana and William James seem often to stay at the level of poetry and perception by delaying fateful in favor of effective integration (WS, *Opus,* 276). Santayana's texts do not offer themselves for "sensational summary" because they are part of "the *douceur de vivre*" (WS, *Opus,* 270). And Santayana might think James's *Principles of Psychology* needs his protection from professionals when he calls it "a literary subject like autobiography or psychological fiction" that can "be treated only poetically," but James, in a mischievous fit of mock sadism, prefers the offensive mood. The reader, he hopes, "begins to be pained here by the extreme vagueness of the terms I am using," by my "intellectual higgledy-piggledyism" (GS, *Char,* 41–42; WJ, *Phil,* 62, xv).[32] And this gleeful confession is much more than the mind defending against itself (WS, *Poems,* 436): "A friend . . . once told me that the thought of my universe made him sick like the sight of the horrible motion of a mass of maggots in their carrion bed" (WJ, *Will,* 136). This lowering of Pluralism to the level of amateur slumming is just as perversely self-delighting: "a turbid, muddled, gothic sort of an affair, without a sweeping out-line and with little pictorial nobility" (WJ, *Plur,* 26). Paradoxically, the abbreviation of philosophic description to political caricature, an unrhymed building out into chaos (Em, 141), through the "buildings-out" of "over-beliefs," the "most interesting and valuable things about a man" (WJ, *Var,* 431, 515), lets us feel more at home in a confluent world. As much as Freud, James played his revisionary puns on the adjective *unheimlich* to turn alienation against the false consolers of conceptual utopias, who excised the gothic intimacy and actuality of temperament (WJ, *Will,* 71). His perception revises, as well, the high metaphysics that had made us uncomfortable with silence, autumn, change, and death. With Santayana, he reappropriates, for the poets who will follow, the diction of divine permanence and perfection to make it live in the vivid air of seasonal rendezvous where temper and spirit are forced to agree that "to be interested in the changing seasons is, in this middling zone, a happier state of mind than to be hopelessly in love with the spring" (GS, *Rel,* 129; WS, *Poems,* 390–91). The descriptions in our honest fictions are revelation (WS, *Poems,* 344) and an agency of "*present* perfecting, a satisfaction in the irremedial poverty of life" that keeps us romanced by nature's night on the road home (WS, *Opus,* 193; *Poems,* 203–4).

With a silent nod to Nietzsche, James raises Emerson's "impulse to believe" to the "will to believe" and makes the possibility of being duped at once a more active risk of and defense against depression (WJ, *Will,* 25; Em, 268). *His* bête noire might be the very skepticism Santayana loved, but both philosophers were both devoted to overcoming aristocratic idealisms and sterile materialisms: "The influence of democracy in promoting pragmatisms is visible in almost every page of William James's writing. There is an impatience of authority, an unwillingness to condemn widespread prejudices, a tendency to decide philosophical questions by putting them to a vote, which contrast curiously with the usual dictatorial tone of philosophic writings" (GS, *Winds,* 124). "Spiritual men . . . may fall into the aristocrat's fallacy; they may forget the infinite animal and vulgar life

32. See the discussion of James's legacy of the vague and superfluous in Poirier, *Poetry and Pragmatism,* 40–75.

which remains quite disjoined, impulsive, and short-winded, but which nevertheless palpitates with joys and sorrows, and makes after all the bulk of moral values in this democratic world" (GS, *Rel,* 214–15). Clearly, in contradistinction to James, Santayana was more worried about being a dupe through hope than through fear (WJ, *Will,* 30). And we are not surprised to hear of his interest in *Beyond the Pleasure Principle* since it psychologically and biologically seemed to justify a regressive urge to peace from the anxieties and goadings of love (GS, *Phil,* 572–73). He obviously identifies with William's brother Henry, who overcame temptations to the passive and moralistic genteel tradition classically, "by understanding it," while William swerved from it into an active "evolutionary view" by which he "entices faith in a new direction," romantically "continuing it into its opposite" (GS, *Winds,* 204, 210).[33]

What is at stake here is the crucial generation of moral energy that comes only with the acknowledgment of the temptations in any given temperament to peace. For Santayana and James, as for Freud, this accompanies the acknowledgment of necessary renunciation so as not to impoverish ideals. If this task is ignored, provisional paralysis, experienced by Santayana in his moments of Platonic reverie and by James in his famous depressive breakdown (through which he invented an identity with an asylum patient and inspired one in Frost's "Servant to Servants") could be continual (WJ, *Var,* 160–61).

Blockage was diabolic seduction in Jonathan Edwards and Saint Teresa, those diagnosticians of spiritual lassitude who so deeply influenced James, like them, a pragmatic scrutinizer of the fruits of a moral life as signs of "what goes on in the single private man" (WJ, *Var,* 20–21, 29). A description of the biological and psychological origins of diseases and dispositions by the thermodynamic metaphor of energy's discharge and damming as often seduces James as Freud: "We need . . . a study of the various types of human being with reference to the different ways in which their energy-reserves may be appealed to and set loose. Biographies and individual experiences of every kind may be drawn here."[34] But while the recognition in Freud climaxes in his energetic rejection of the infantilism of the oceanic feeling in *Civilization and Its Discontents,* it crests in James with the equally energetic acceptance of the varieties of religious experience that reunite psychology and spirit: "although all the special manifestations of religion may have been absurd (I mean its creeds and theories), yet the life of it as a whole is mankind's most important function" (WJ, *Ltrs,* 187). The

---

33. See Posnock, *Trial,* 206–8.

34. George Santayana, *Reason in Common Sense,* 173; henceforth cited in the text as GS, *Sense.* WJ, *Var,* 51. William James, *The Writings of William James,* 683; henceforth cited in the text as WJ, *Writ.*

recovery from depression makes use of the Puritan diction that counts *abulia,* a disjunction of vision and action, as a moral sin and sex as a sublimation of spirit (WJ, *Var,* 10–13; *Writ,* 703): "The man who lives in his religious centre of personal energy, and is actuated by spiritual enthusiasms, differs from his previous carnal self in perfectly definite ways. The new ardor which burns in his breast consumes in its glow the lower 'noes' which formerly beset him, and keeps him immune against infection from the entire groveling portion of his nature. Magnanimities once impossible are now easy" (WJ, *Var,* 267).

The dangers of excessive or deviant discharge are recorded, as they are morally discriminated in the pages of Santayana and humorously punished in the poems of Frost and Stevens, but for James "volitional effort" almost seems moral enough if it works for energy (WJ, *Writ,* 699). Because his temperament was known in all its tendencies to depression, its need for compensatory postures of enthusiasm is also known. Santayana characterizes the James temper and its uses for pragmatism by reminding us, once again, that the great liberator of primary energy is the imagined life: "The *sense* of bounding over the waves, the *sense* of being on an adventurous voyage, was the living fact; the rest was dead reckoning. Where one's gift is, there will one's faith be also; and to this poet appearance was the only reality" (GS, *Char,* 43–44). Santayana supports, of course, the transposition of moral emphasis to the word *sense* since it is the agent of literary psychology, the perception by which we read our "dreamful, passionate, dramatic, and significative" selves into an "always incipient cosmos" (WS, *Opus,* 140). He could use the aesthetically legitimate protection and James the morally legitimate hope proffered by some philosophic systems, but not when they were hypostatized beyond the "expressible in literature and talk" (GS, *Char,* 45). Perception is a moral agent for both philosophers because it confesses to being only instrumental, and James's biologizing of the will to believe actually frees it from Darwinian and Freudian determinism because, essentially pragmatic, it is directed against the abulic pathos of a religion that had, for so long, kept us waiting for a pitying grace or merciful reward (WJ, *Var,* 142, 346).

If James was obsessed with immortality, we might surmise, it was because he wanted more and more of life; if Santayana, on the other hand, was drawn to perfection, it was because he wanted less and less. What bothers Santayana most in James is an overgenerous tolerance accorded any faith, so that he might "make us unmindful of the moral and educative responsibilities" of aesthetic nobility, when even dramatists "let the audience perceive who is good and who bad, who wise and who foolish" (GS, *Char,* 48). We feel the James behind Santayana's version of Browning's barbaric artistic temperament that blocks him from discriminating between exuberances. Santayana's Browning preferred to believe "that life is an adventure, not a discipline; that the exercise of energy is the absolute good, irrespective of motives or of consequences." He swings from one extravagance to another, never "calling thought home," where poetic piety would bring it to safety (GS, *Interp*, 125–27; *Rel*, 186).

When Santayana calls James a "spirited rather than a spiritual man," he tries to rescue him from a compulsive American charity that threatened to thin his own thick world of values as thoroughly as did overexclusive theologies (GS, *Char*, 52). The equilibrium sought by Santayana's temper, which dreaded exhaustion from too much moral responsibility to his adopted republic, might be achieved through this conviction addressed to James: "to be boosted by an illusion is not to live better than to live in harmony with the truth; it is not nearly so safe, not nearly so sweet, and not nearly so fruitful" (GS, *Char*, 53–54). The will to believe had to be harnessed to the will to discriminate between beliefs. Santayana makes his aesthetic skepticism toward the world he works in and his Platonic longing for the world he imagines suffer the instrumentality of a pragmatism that qualifies *the Truth* at least as much as does the frenetic hopefulness of James's will to believe. James, on the other hand, was wary that too judicious a discrimination of religious imagination, complemented by an overfine literary one, might keep Santayana from the passionate preferences he handled with kid gloves.

IV. The Conversation Bequeathed: Frost and Stevens

The legitimating of the temperamental need for safety in Santayana by circumscribing James's need for hope finds a new host in his student Frost, who, if he favored the authority given James's will to believe and thought Santayana's "all is illusion" too sad, also admitted he was drawn to *Robinson Crusoe*'s representation of how the "limited can make snug in the limitless" (RF, *P&P*, 388, 355). It is true that James, in listing the great advantages of the life of religion, an act that might temperamentally be set against Nietzsche's listing of the disadvantages to be borne by the new "immoralists" with the loss of even a dead Christianity, couples the agency of energy with "an assurance of safety and a temper of peace" (WJ, *Var*, 486). There is no question that James's temperamental choice of pragmatic pluralism, a choice that calls us home from the *Unheimlichkeit* of manic monisms, gave Frost a primary legacy, the joy of extravagant meditation on a star in a stoneboat and the belief in belief as virtual action. But the poet also honored Santayana's piety that "saves speculative and emotional life from extravagance" (GS, *Rel*, 185–86).[35] If poetry is "a sort of extrava-

35. For a discussion of "extravagance" as it comes into Frost, especially in this poem,

gance" pushed by what Santayana called our "passionate preference" and James our "passional tendencies and volitions" that "run before and after belief," it is also, for Frost, what tames an "extravagant universe" if we allow ourselves to be "at home" in the metaphor and, in fact, is "enthusiasm tamed by metaphor" (RF, *P&P*, 448, 332; WJ, *Will*, 19–20; RF, *P&P*, 331–32, 334, 447).

Surely Frost was attracted to the Jamesian aphorism: "All 'homes' are in finite experience; finite experience as such is homeless" (WJ, *Prag*, 125). But Frost's obsession with the pole of safety takes on the color of Santayana's fear of barbarism. Often it seems to derive from the child's superstitious need to appease the gods for his hubristic stabs at bravado and to protect against the invasive disturbance of the accident and calamity so prevalent in his own life. Because the James and Santayana in Frost vigorously test each other, often with ironic animus, the frequent and humorous Santayana fantasy of a "world safe for art" might be a secret Jamesian hope for an art powerful enough and bold enough to play in a world that seems "a wild place" (RF, *P&P*, 359–60). The exuberance of metaphor that rides us out on its qualifying and far-fetching syntax of "as if" and "something like" ultimately breaks down and educates us to ride it back home (RF, *Writing*, 146; *P&P*, 334). This "luminous flittering" is the testing that, finally, trains us to measure. The form that "must stroke faith the right way" to spare us from "the larger excruciations" of any age goes slumming with the Jamesian *more* that relativizes the absolute for the sake of a new superlative (RF, *P&P*, 344). Stevens quips: "The notion of absolutes is relative"; and Frost: "To me any little form I assert" is "to be considered for how much more it is than nothing. If I were a Platonist I should have to consider it, I suppose, for how much less it is than everything" (WS, *Opus*, 185; RF, *P&P*, 345). A poem Frost claims begins in extravagance is a fine example of his hedging: "He would declare and could himself believe" (RF, *P&P*, 451); this is the move that guarantees his best moral and aesthetic energies.

Frost is fierce about the need to acknowledge the temperament that, in handling its "ideas and deeds," seeks both energy and protection. If these urges are in disequilibrium, the poet suffers the poverty of mere necessity, of temperament as fate: "Mind you if he is down-spirited it will be all he can do to have the ideas without the carriage. The style is out of his superfluity" (RF, *P&P*, 299). The depression derives from the refusal to let temperament tease spirit. The slumming would set up the delightful and necessary qualification of spirit's progressive absolute—"the mind skating circles round itself as it moves forward" (RF, *P&P*, 298–99). This is a ver-

---

see Richard Poirier, *Robert Frost* and *Poetry and Pragmatism*, 411–75, and Lentricchia, *Robert Frost*.

sion of Stevens's faith that the mind, by its forms, protects us against itself (WS, *Opus,* 199). For both poets, the slumming of spirit assures responsiveness to temperament's role in making poems out of the "stresses" the poet "invites" and those he "avoids" and out of the game of both disarming and protecting competitors by "seeming to have heard and done justice to [their] side" (WS, *Essays,* 122; RF, *P&P,* 299).

James warns us that the athletic drive toward the expression of energy breaks down in the moralist, like the ride on metaphor, and needs to direct itself to a sufficing faith that assures the continual ambulation between the defensive and aggressive moods, protecting and stirring temperament (WJ, *Prag,* 245). He reminds us that metamorphosis of mood from "dull submission" to "welcome" occurs only in those poets and philosophers whose bearing toward ideas is stirred to ideal action against resistance, the Emersonian otherness of the world of competing tempers in and between selves. Aggressive and embattled metaphors against mystic mergings and pathetic fallacies march through the pages of the American philosophers and poets. James imagines a world that willingly "suffers human violence" as "man *engenders* truths upon it"; Frost and Stevens register a rougher meeting. If good writing comes, for Frost, from "making the sentences talk to each other as two or more speakers do in drama," it must make them suffer, like temperament and spirit, the brutal context of the realism of "strained relations" between meter and accent: "I like to drag and break the intonation across the meter as waves first comb and then break stumbling on the shingle" (WJ, *Var,* 41; *Prag,* 123; RF, *Ltrs,* 427, 128). This roughness, the sense of pitching into commitment that makes "strongly spent . . . synonymous with kept," might be the fight Frost needs "to keep [him]self as [he] wanted to be" in a "world much of which [he] didn't love," a world of "alien entanglements" (RF, *P&P,* 401; *Ltrs,* 202). Stevens puts it in a way that complements the recurrent war metaphor in his poems: "Perhaps poetry, instead of being the rather meaningless transmutation of reality, is a combat with it; and perhaps the thing to do when one keeps saying that life is a dull life is to pick a fight with reality" (WS, *Ltrs,* 620–21). Nothing can pick a fight better than temperament with a reality that would ignore it, the catalyst engendering "a violence from within that protects us from a violence without . . . the imagination pressing back against the pressure of reality," its "rage of form and colour" against the "rage of the world" (WS, *Essays,* 34, 36). Only because the mind's imagination can be "the most terrible force in the world" can it "defend us against terror" (WS, *Opus,* 199). Frost supports Stevens's notion of the possible poet as a resister and shaper when he calls him "the brute who can knock the corners off the marble block and drag the unbedded beauty out of bed" (RF, *P&P,* 359).

By imagining forth an aggressive fiction of identity against the pathetic fallacy of a literal merging in "Credences of Summer," "Without evasion by a single metaphor" (WS, *Poems*, 373), could the poet expose the temptation to pathos lurking in the poem's necessary evasion of definition, flush it out from behind its refuge, an undialectical design of self-protection? From his marginal position he could, perhaps, gain a compensatory energy of imagination by acknowledging the loss, in Santayana's mode, of an old, culturally energetic context: "The savage assailant of life who uses literature as a weapon just does not exist, any more than the savage lover of life exists" (WS, *Ltrs*, 624). In an ironic age, a lull "between seasons of steady blowing," in which Santayana's poet of "double insight," as an inquisitor of his contemporary reality and an agent of new perception, is still in limbo, the humor that both defends and attacks cannot, as Kafka taught us, let itself defeat the world.[36] But a drama of contrary mood in poem after poem might cast the new temperamental poet into a more than tolerable and everlasting purgatory:

> He never supposed
> That he might be truth, himself, or part of it,
> That the things that he rejected might be part
> And the irregular turquoise, part, the perceptible blue
> Grown denser, part, the eye so touched, so played
> Upon by clouds, the ear so magnified
> By thunder, parts, and all these things together,
> Parts, and more things, parts.
>
> (WS, *Poems*, 242)

> And though one says that one is part of everything,
>
> There is a conflict, there is a resistance involved;
> And being part is an exertion that declines:
> One feels the life of that which gives life as it is.
>
> (WS, *Opus*, 123)

The separations and mergings practiced by Romantic idealisms, pathetic monisms, the "old nostalgias," forced by logic's implicit dualism that would pan for "Reality explained," prevent us from "our only opportunity of making the god's acquaintance," as he might be, surging out of temperament's weather: "passions of rain, or moods in falling snow; / Grievings in loneliness, or unsubdued / Elations when the forest blooms; gusty / Emotions on wet roads on autumn nights" (WS, *Poems*, 322; WJ, *Will*, 31; WS, *Poems*, 67). James's tireless dialectical drama of energy and protection that helps

36. GS, *Winds*, 24; WS, *Essays*, 34. George Santayana, *Three Philosophical Poets*, 190–91; henceforth cited in the text as GS, *3 Poets*.

us to experience difficulties as "disappointments and uncertainties . . . not intellectual contradictions" (WJ, *Essays,* 69) is played out in the only life in which we "volitionally feel at home" (WJ, *Will,* 101), where Eden is not what James dreaded, a boring climax of Beyond (WJ, *Will,* 130), or Stevens, a terrifyingly unanalogous place (WS, *Essays,* 76; *Poems,* 69), but the stage "from which the rationalists seek in vain to expel us," to "derealize" the "genuineness of each particular moment in which we insensibly feel the squeeze of this world's life, as we actually do work here, or work is done upon us" (WJ, *Phil,* 60).

The poverty of dualism that had kept the gossipers starving in mystical monism's "glut of oneness" (WJ, *Prag,* 74) now calls out a willful "poverty" of impurity, a pluralism within and without that wars against the designs of disjunction and antithesis in favor of those of conjunction and apposition. The refusal to close off the rich ambiguity of competing rights, impulses, anxieties, in an open world, of the tensions between apology and assertion in ourselves, between each other, with nature, inspires the poet to justify himself against the tramps in mud-time, but only by means of a partial *story* rooted in animal faith and wearing the costume of principle:

> My object in living is to unite
> My avocation and my vocation
> As my two eyes make one in sight.
> (RF, *Poems,* 277)

Love and need, work and play, stir temperament, not ideology, to write poems out of animus that, fringing all fact with feeling, engender James's favorite hybrid: "the sweetest dream that labor knows" (RF, *Poems,* 17). How Frost must have loved the passage in James's *Principles of Psychology* that speaks of the stubborn resistance to the appropriation of the preferred things and tasks that mark our identity, making us feel—in an image, like so many, borrowed from his father—that "we are all assimilated to the tramps . . . we despise" (WJ, *Writ,* 45). The assimilation of spirit by matter, practiced by materialisms, and of matter by spirit, practiced by idealisms, is subtly prevented by the revisionary poetry that *speaks* matter in terms of spirit (RF, *P&P,* 357). Frost's "After Apple-Picking" suggests all the Platonic temptations, but its major drama is the refusal of transcendence, the courting of anti-Platonic "compenetration" (WJ, *Prag,* 257), physics and metaphysics teasing each other into and out of climactic fulfillment, into and out of dream and waking, the natural and interested emanations of animal faith caricatured by a woodchuck. "Versed in country things," the weather of perception, the most "unphilosophical reality," allows us to tease pathetic fallacies because it does not need them (RF, *Poems,* 241; WJ, *Prag,* 85; WS, *Ltrs,* 394). For the birds there is "really nothing sad" about ruins, and for the possible poet, nothing sad about a syntax that uses negatives to keep the universe one we could "merely enjoy" (WS, *Poems,* 430):

> But though they rejoiced in the nest they kept,
> One had to be versed in country things
> Not to believe the phoebes wept.
>
> (RF, *Poems,* 242)

Playfully correcting Santayana, Frost cures the philosophy of "all was illusion" by this revision: "And I decided false illusion would be the truth; two negatives make an affirmative" (RF, "Art," 108). But if the poet refuses to be an "unaffected man in a negative light" (WS, *Poems,* 393), he must seize upon a felt syntax of the possible that keeps the Hegelian "negative" from leading us to an idealistic and totalitarian climax. Against the "nothing but" of positivist and idealist philosophies (WJ, *Prag,* 15), against the "negatives that haunt our ideals here below" and are, themselves, "negated in the absolutely Real" (WJ, *Prag,* 124–25, 126), Frost, in league with James, Santayana, Stevens, sets up obsessively doubled negatives and qualifying adverbs of mere sufficiency to cancel the purification by the absolute of the relative world, the "one world complete in any size / That I am like to compass" (RF, *Poems,* 174), the world kept open by the first line of "Star in a Stoneboat," the last lines of "Never Again Would Bird Song Be the Same," "The Onset," "Come In," "Desert Places," "The Snow-Man," the bold third line of "Le Monocle de mon Oncle."

Primordial perception disturbs the "fanatic syntax" (WJ, *Var,* 341) of barren, unstoried abstractions that make "silhouettes of our dreams" (GS, *Sense,* 178), dreams that should be free to play with the vivid caricaturing of self in the bodies of familiar citizens of the Rock. Instead of an anachronistic "idealization by proxy" of dead fathers, the vivid imaginings of animal faith conceiving instrumental nicknames of perception are projected from the half-waking, half-dreaming mind that refuses the nourishment of fallacies not proud enough to leave fictions unpathetic and not humble enough to accept the inevitability of illusion (GS, *Interp,* 158; WJ, *Prag,* 121). If we are hyperconscious in the age of hard and soft sciences, between supreme fictions, "in a place / That is not our own and, much more, not ourselves" (WS, *Poems,* 383; *Ltrs,* 444), at least the Realpolitik of its prophets—Darwin, Marx, Freud—has helped us to realize that "the prevalent mood of mankind has changed" and has begun "dreaming in a different key" (GS, *Phil,* 475). They exposed the "maladjustment between the imagination and reality" brought on by the refusal to give up dead gods (WS, *Essays,* 13), a necessary abdication if mankind is to dream itself dramatically free of abulia that "never gets its voice out of the minor key" into the pitch of living spirit (WJ, *Writ,* 703). As "authors of genuine novelty" (WJ, *Phil*, 75) we can now partake of Emerson's oblique power that shuffles us from minor toward major (Em, 265). This provisional position might be our nearest approach to the Greeks who "would have despised a life set wholly in a minor key" (WJ, *Var*, 142). No longer can rich pathetic fallacies, as in a savage day of faith, shake us out of our "servile speech and imaginative poverty"; on the contrary, our diction of value, if it remains attached to old metaphysical designs and Romantic habits, "must either be impoverished to remain sincere, or become artificial to remain adequate" (GS, *Interp*, 159, 38). The great advantage in recognizing that what the young crave, a philosophy with "more of the temperament of life" even if it comes "at some cost of logical rigor and formal purity" (WJ, *Essays*, 21), is the beginning of pragmatic wisdom that reads courageously our diminished environment and refuses to "blame" the "minor bird" "for his key" or to silence him in the name of a major song (RF, *Poems*, 120, 251).

If Christianity furnished us once with a suffering "mythology loaded with pathos" in response to the cravings of its age, with time it has become, for almost all diagnosticians of the modern lull between seasons, "the uncourageous genesis" of a "self-pity" stirred out of selfishness and apathy only by the moral exercise of comparative cartooning:

> The fault lies with an over-human god,
> Who by sympathy has made himself a man
> . . . .
> If only he would not pity us so much,
> Weaken our fate, relieve us of woe both great
> And small, a constant fellow of destiny,
>
> A too human god, self-pity's kin
> And uncourageous genesis . . . It seems
> As if the health of the world might be enough.
>   (WS, *Poems*, 315)

When, in a characteristically modern move, Stevens lowers moral terms from "goodness" to "health" evidenced by his "enoughs" and "merelys," an echo of Santayana's "suffice," itself a revision of Hegel's "adequate," he achieves, in a minor age, the major language of live hypothesis, the language of pluralism's spirited, temperamental, and jousting "over-beliefs" set against the collective or isolating under-beliefs of Darwin, Marx, and Freud (WJ, *Var*, 519; cf. GS, *Winds*, 7). The new unfanatical syntax waves "a definitive good-by to dogmatic theology" from the pages of James into the poems of Stevens (WJ, *Var*, 448) and gains a larger landscape that profits from the continuity, in the moody body, of the real and ideal worlds. Any recourse to the "false projection of sentiment" by which we "soak

Nature with our own feeling, and then celebrate her tender sympathy with our moral being," is rendered dangerously dull and reductive by its repression of competing projections out of the clash of temperaments (GS, *Interp*, 158). That mere tautology, a faked expansion, assailed in its divine aspect by Feuerbach, Marx, and Freud, actually *disconnects* the believer from "a wider self" that is "continuous with a *more* of the same quality which is operative in the universe outside of him and which he can keep in working touch with" (WJ, *Plur*, 139). Only a distrust of the dramatic personality of imagination as a vigorous and morally discriminating part of reality engenders the inverted landscapes of the Beyond that is, in fact, as Nietzsche tirelessly taught, "the refuge of poetical selfishness" (GS, *Interp*, 17).

When the poet vigorously makes the "visible a little hard to see," he counters the escapist division of the real from the unreal, fact from ideal, temperament from divine imagination, what Santayana calls the absolute "poverty of the imagination, when left alone."[37] The philosopher caps the claim with the favorite pragmatist metaphor of appetite, passed on to Stevens: "The hunger of the soul will gnaw its own emptiness forever" when we fail to "taste at the root of the tongue the unreal of what is real" (GS, *Interp*, 165; WS, *Poems*, 313). What Stevens names the "false imagination" becomes a "flatterer of things instead of the principle of their ideal correction" (WS, *Essays*, 73; GS, *Interp*, 12). And when the citizen of the Rock preaches a dead belief, as in the passage from Platonism to Neo-Platonism, instead of guessing out a living faith from temperamental need and interest, he kills, in Santayana's persuasion, the moral imagination necessary for a living culture: "For an ideal is not ideal if it is the ideal of nothing. In that case it is only a ghostly existence, with no more moral significance or authority in relation to the observer than has any happy creature which may happen to exist somewhere in the unknown reaches of the universe" (GS, *Rel*, 134–35). That kind of conviction is behind James's apparent anthropomorphizing of God by forcing him into the vivid atmosphere of clashing tempers from which he has been removed by monistic derealizers of our life on earth:

> God . . . must be conceived under the form of a mental personality. The personality need not be determined intrinsically any further than is involved in the . . . recognition of our dispositions toward those things, the things themselves being all good and righteous things. But, extrinsically considered, so to speak, God's personality is to be regarded, like any other personality, as something

---

37. This mystifying of reality to deepen it probably owes something to Ruskin's analysis of Turner in "Of Turnerian Mystery," *Modern Painters*, 4:64–78. See also Ruskin's discussion of the marginality of the picturesque in *The Seven Lamps of Architecture*, chap. 6. For a review and discussion of a longer history of American negative structures see Terence Martin, "The Negative Structure of American Literature."

lying outside of my own and other than me, and whose existence I simply come upon and find. (WJ, *Will,* 98)

What he gives to Stevens is supreme value for the way to *meet* the God; such a place of transition, like the street that hosted Santayana's jibe about religious slumming, cannot, by its syntactical nature, suppress one or another of the jousting pairs that have for so long been ranged in hierarchical orders.

The obsessive "as if" that assures the continuity of the real and the unreal to philosopher and poet alike sponsors the fictions that "resist the intelligence / Almost successfully" (WS, *Poems,* 350). The poets' obsession with landscapes only half-visible or holographically remembered, imagined, is carried by the syntax of James's possible that makes fact at once a brute resister and felt conductor of our larger feelings, insured against both sentimentality and desertion. As much as his brother, who would not let his characters stay in landscapes "clipped, straight-edged and artificial" (WJ, *Essays,* 21), cleared of needs, tempers, self-idealizing desires, and self-confronting facts, William James held out against too easy a melting into the universe. That is why his fact holds out "blankly, brutally and blindly, against the universal deliquescence of the ideal and real worlds, their melting into systems, logical relations which the Absolute Logic demands" (WJ, *Essays,* 140). The comparative "more," a key evaluative term in James's ambulatory meetings by transition, gains superlative power in refusing to close by conception or settle by synthesis. The distracting certainty of Frost's aphorisms needs to be aesthetically teased by the questioning context that holds them even as one rationalizing temperamental philosopher needs to be psychologically met by his competitor: "What had how long it takes a birch to rot / To do with what was in the darkened parlor?" (RF, *Poems,* 54). The great swelling of the world felt through new perception comes through liberation from all that promised to swell it by dividing its philosophies, by keeping them from guessing at each other. When James returns to religion the temperament it had curtailed, he recovers for us, "the strong man vaguely seen" (WS, *Poems,* 204), a thrilling dimension immune to those bullying theories that were "quite careless of their bearing on human anxieties and fates" (WJ, *Var,* 491) and quite smug in their suppression of the dialectical drama of test and temptation. The transitive, quantitative, and comparative "more" assumes a qualitative moral force against the measure of "good" or "most" that had squeezed our "thin" and "spended hearts." Here is the new scene in which we might bathe in the mists "Like a man without a doctrine" (WS, *Poems,* 424, 204–5): "Our fields of experience have no more definite boundaries than have our fields of view. Both are fringed forever by a *more* that continually develops, and that continuously supersedes them as life proceeds" (WJ, *Essays,* 35). This "more" insists upon the cohabitation of fact and imagination, for when we are at the end of one we are, as well, at the end of the other (WS, *Essays,* 60; *Opus,* 200; Em, 36) The field of foraging animal faith is "a conscious field *plus* its object as felt or thought of *plus* an attitude towards the object *plus* the sense of a self to whom the attitude belongs" (WJ, *Var,* 499).

The staggered Jamesian "more," which becomes the constant qualifying incremental relative superlative of Stevens's new-come worlds, bellows poem after poem:

> The trumpet of morning blows in the clouds and through
> The sky. It is the visible announced,
> It is the more than visible, the more
> Than sharp, illustrious scene . . .
>
> (WS, *Poems,* 376)

"We never arrive intellectually" at the "most," but "emotionally we arrive constantly as in poetry, happiness, high mountains, vistas" (WS, *Opus,* 198). The major man arrives, projected out of the personal and collective need of the times, is called out by temperament, and then calls out "our own higher self" (WJ, *Var,* 510).

The religious task of thinking ourselves larger in a larger world would have "abstraction blooded" read us back into the "poem of life" and all its facts then take on "color . . . shape and the size of things as they are," speak "the feeling for them, which was what they had lacked" (WS, *Poems,* 385, 424). Major man is made of the comparative building out from temperament to a provisional superlative that, by remaining subject to a dominating "as if," returns the "Beyond" to reality, the poet to his poems by which he is both most himself and most ourselves, since we are "conceived" in his "conceits" (WS, *Poems,* 195). Major men are

> characters beyond
> Reality, composed thereof. They are
> The fictive man created out of men.
> They are men but artificial men. They are
> Nothing in which it is not possible
> To believe, more than the casual hero, more
> Than Tartuffe as myth, the most Molière,
> The easy projection long prohibited.
>
> (WS, *Poems,* 335)

Frost's use of the relative sublime, "The Most of It," by its attachment to the state of dialogue of contraries that "is most us" (RF, *Poems,* 260), also mocks the old prohibiting dead measures of theology and the Wordsworthian sublime of "something" but gives, with the "as ifs" and "something likes," a revelation that survives ironic reduction:

> "This is all," they sighed,
> "Good-night to woods." But not so; there was more.
> . . . .
> *"This,* then, is all. What more is there to ask?"
> But no, not yet.
> . . . .
> "This *must* be all." It was all. Still they stood,
> A great wave from it going over them,
> As if the earth in one unlooked for favor
> Had made them certain earth returned their love.
> (RF, *Poems,* 229)

The final lines of "All Revelation" and "For Once, Then, Something" honor as much our craving as they scorn its tendency to perversions of pathos. The marginal and sprawling posture of the felt syntax of a world in which fact is continuous with feeling yields the saving self-ironies inherent in the "ever not quites" of comparative temperament (WJ, *Plur,* 145) and in the habit of "saying something that's just the edge of something more" (RF, *P&P,* 298).

The old metaphysical syntax of "either/or," "nothing but," cannot serve the new perception constantly engaged in earning provisional ascents by common caricature, taking conjunctions at their face value, namely rhetorically: "consider, for example, such conjunctions as 'and,' 'with,' 'near,' *'plus,'* 'towards.' While we live in such conjunctions our state is one of *transition* in the most literal sense. We are expectant of a 'more' to come, and before the more *has* come, the transition, nevertheless, is directed *towards* it" (WJ, *Essays,* 120). This is the familiar drama played out by the competing philosopher crossing the street to deliver his boutade. Even in the anecdote, the adverb of direction is stressed because the witty exchange *is* transition. Perhaps the most important of James's remodelings for the pragmatic poets is his willingness to use his syntax to relocate us in the post-Darwinian universe, his insistence on investing the passionate ethical as well as epistemological authority of old theologies of terms in a new theology of transitions (WJ, *Essays,* 42). The felt adverbial prepositions that receive such special emphasis in the poets, the moving markers of our relocation, the "towards" and "downwards," retain the feeling of our metaphysical craving while refusing its translation into a transcendental beyond. The fictively revised "beyond" and "part of" in Stevens that continuously connect this craving with the necessary angel of the earth make us energetic citizens in a new and rich maze, itself recovered from its infernal Miltonic doom (WJ, *Will,* 63).

The lure of the temptation to synthesis is exhibited in James's Hegel, who forgot that the life he finally put into balance must remain "something always off its balance, something in transition, something that shoots out of a darkness through a dawn into a brightness that we *feel* to be the dawn fulfilled" (WJ, *Plur,* 128; Em, 158). A father of nineteenth-century evolutionary immanence, Hegel admirably plants himself as "a naively observant man" in "the empirical flux of things and gets the impression of what happens. His mind is in very truth impressionistic" (WJ, *Plur,* 44). And we can grasp his vision if we put ourselves "at the animating center," that dialectical place in which we move in tragic transitions between inadequate courtships of spirit and temperament. But speculative philosophy sells out its potential humility of wonder when it makes an absolute of "adequate," literalizes it not by a "passionate preference" but by "a perverse preference for the use of technical and logical jargon" (WJ, *Plur,* 86–87). The value, finally, is refused to the transition, and to the temperament of individuals blanched out into world-historical figures and moved not by the urgings of animal faith in an open universe but by history's necessity.

If the life dominated by temperament was one, for Emerson, in which we sprawl and sin (Em, 139), and one for T. S. Eliot's Prufrock in which we sprawl and are pinned, for the possible philosophers it was one that could, in both the best and worst of Emersonian moods, conduct our "gossip" of "the eternal politics" (Em, 272). It is one that, like Stevens's Socrates, reclines in "a hostile and a fatal world" (WS, *Opus,* 279) coaxing down the envy of a bodiless paradise:

> Perhaps,
> After death, the non-physical people, in paradise,
> Itself non-physical, may, by chance, observe
> The green corn gleaming and experience
> The minor of what we feel. The adventurer
> In humanity has not conceived of a race
> Completely physical in a physical world.
> The green corn gleams and the metaphysicals
> Lie sprawling in majors of the August heat,
> The rotund emotions, paradise unknown.
>> (WS, *Poems,* 325)

James had prepared for this imagination when he forced philosophy to posture against expectation: "Philosophy, you will say, doesn't lie flat on its belly in the middle of experience, in the very thick of its sand and gravel . . . never getting a peep at anything from above. Philosophy is essentially the vision of things from above" (WJ, *Plur,* 125).

That old vision is one that can never imagine the majors by acknowledging the minors of the human situation and its adventures. Frost gives but a slightly different version of the new sprawl: "My own idea of poetry isn't of its climbing on top of the earth, nor of its standing on top of the earth, but of its reclining on top of the earth and giving way to its moods. Like a spoiled actress, you know, the day after she has been on the stage, reclining on top of the world and giving way to her moods" (RF, *P&P,* 119). It is this intimate, vulgar, vulnerable posture that forces the noble riders of Platonic longings to dismount, slum, like Frost's movie star, in contexts of gay seasonal gossip, contexts of both men and their gods. What has been heard as foreign foppishness in Stevens's diction might instead be the long-exiled piety bringing the extravagance of "trite conceptions designated by current words" home to the "sensuous qualities out of which those conceptions were originally put together" (GS, *Interp,* 155–56). If Santayana's resignation to the medium of illusion made him seem sad to Frost, it more often fostered in Stevens the continually qualified gospel of a "fluent mundo" (WS, *Poems,* 407). The philosopher speaks of the shock that stuns us, even offends us, like the holy parables, when we hear, as if for the first time, nature flaunting its "rich vocabulary" and find ourselves "sometimes speaking a language, or enjoying a syntax which [we] never heard at home" (GS, *Phil,* 423). The new posture in the "imperfect" of our "paradise" (WS, *Poems,* 194) assures us that we can sometimes guiltlessly hear the temperamental "tootings at the weddings of the soul" (WS, *Poems,* 222), but only by recoining the "flawed words and stubborn sounds" of our conditioned animal faith, "hot in us," into "paradisal parlance new" (WS, *Poems,* 194, 475). The gaiety of nature's language cannot sound native until we choose the poverty of our native situation rather than receive it as fate (WS, *Poems,* 322).

The historical bankruptcy of a generation made "sick with space" (RF, *Poems,* 352) and "experiencing essential poverty in spite of fortune" (WS, *Essays,* 171) is homeopathically confronted in the literature of its representative philosophers and poets by creative entrenchment, a "decreation" that activates, like psychoanalytic therapy, the renunciation that would otherwise be only necessary (WS, *Essays,* 174). Amateur notes toward supreme fictions might suffice as the script of revelation when change, pleasure, blooded thought, chase off the fixed, dour, pale poverty of pity, appeasement, grace that had cleared animal faith of its active temperamental curiosity. Renunciation is not a spiritual climax but a constant and instinctive rhythm of our expressive creation: "The doctrine that all moralities equally are but expressions of animal life is a tremendous dogma, at once blessing and purging all mortal passions; and the conviction that there can be no knowledge save animal faith positing external facts, and that this science is but a human symbol for those facts, also has an immense final-ity: the renunciation and the assurance in it are both radical and both invincible" (GS, *Phil,* 483). The poet who blesses and purges the world's poverty, as "prince of the proverbs of pure poverty" vulnerable to artificial poverties of escape, needs to go beyond the patience with his "own frosts and negations" urged by Emerson (WS, *Poems,* 320; Em, 189). An active life of reason, as Santayana defines it, of the discrimination of illusions and poverties, "far from creating the partial renunciation and proportionate sacrifices which it imposes, really minimizes them by making them voluntary and fruitful" (GS, *Sense,* 173). When the poet manages by "cognitive abstention" and acute attention to almost see the world as an ignorant man, he realizes for us that "retrenchment has its rewards" (GS, *Phil,* 394); and by virtue of turning his back on the "empty heaven" and "its hymns" (WS, *Poems,* 167) he keeps the chatter going between need and essence:

> Need makes
> The right to use. Need names on its breath
> Categories of bleak necessity,
> Which, just to name, is to create
> A help, a right to help, a right
> To know what helps and to attain,
> By right of knowing, another plane.
>
> (WS, *Opus,* 130–31)

Impoverishing ideals of supernatural utopias whose moralities are merely "irresponsible rules" and whose results are merely "magical and undeserved happiness" (GS, *Sense,* 173) cannot engage the energy that works temperament's poverty into poetry's affluence in poverty, the "chiefest embracing of all wealth" (WS, *Opus,* 130; *Poems,* 532–33).

The rising out of chosen poverty that allows us to feel part of an "always incipient cosmos" is radiantly responsive not only to the way we live in the universe but also to the educating task of prospective building out against the retrospective stability of conceptual ordering. This "remodelling," as James calls it, is the dramatic vocation of consciousness, and the daily conversion of chaos to cosmos is the task passed on to their representative poets, the passionate "Connoisseur(s) of Chaos" (WJ, *Will,* 95; *Prag,* 66; cf. GS, *Phil,* 423–24; *Interp,* 147–49; WS, *Poems,* 215). The amateur thinkers "without final thoughts," mere "things of shreds and patches," must gossip into poetry the chaos of a "constellation" felt as "patches and pitches" (WS, *Opus,* 140; GS, *Interp,* 104; WJ, *Prag,* 83; GS, *Sense,* 37). Frost, we remember, defined gossip as the "height of imagination" for its power to guess past barriers, and Stevens adds the building metaphor dear to the philosophers who continually insisted that "Openness, too, is a form of architecture": "When does a building stop being a product of the reason and become a product of the imagination? If we raise a building to an imaginative height, then the building becomes an imaginative building since height in itself is imaginative" (WS, *Essays*, 150). This is an identification theologians might forget, but not the philosophers of animal faith who know the earth is a body, not a building. The job of soothing the latest "maladjustment between the imagination and reality" (WS, *Essays*, 33) starts in the acknowledgment of the continual genesis of spirit in marginal temperamentalism, the continual connection between the bearing of our bodies and our books. The imaginative impurity of the poem's gossip prevents poetic selfishness by forcing the temperament to work for the welfare of the whole race and to keep all synthetic, statistical, "sociological," "treadmilled averages" from describing us, for they are "the most pernicious and immoral of fatalisms" (WJ, *Will*, 185, 195, 262). The possible poet of double insight must know the race in all its natural and artificial poverty, through his own temperament, to keep us "from spoiling our science by making it fantastic and our dreams by making them obligatory" (GS, *3 Poets*, 190).

Stevens poses the modern question: "At what level of the truth" shall the possible poet "compose his poems?" (WS, *Essays* 62); he calibrates it in the poems:

> To say more than human things with human voice,
> That cannot be; to say human things with more
> Than human voice, that, also, cannot be:
> To speak humanly from the height or from the depth
> Of human things, that is acutest speech.
>
> (WS, *Poems*, 300)

James associated the desire and capacity to speak as a "wider thinker" (WJ, *Var*, 160) with the religious impulse, and Stevens received it as Santayana's major measure of breadth. The poet's great poem on the "old philosopher in Rome" might well have been inspired by Santayana's insistent recognition that we grow larger by thinking ourselves large (GS, *Rel*, 275) since thinking is "the most vital way ... of living" (GS, *Phil*, 586) when it exercises the "mores" of gossiping tempers. This is a problem for worn-out humanisms not in love with even healthy mythologies (WS, *Ltrs*, 448). We need something more, a fiction that can move and persuade a community of readers to want to be read forth by a Major Man and his poet into the widest world where even "different men's headaches may become confluent or co-conscious" (WJ, *Prag*, 264). Emerson's central poet who "stands among partial men for the complete man" is "more himself than he is" because his *expression* doubles us as it makes him the "most Molière" (Em, 223; WS, *Poems*, 335). James and Santayana call out their poets from their "momentary margin[s]" (WJ, *Plur*, 131) where they move "to and fro," spinning out a living language to connect their "gibberish" to that of the "vulgate" (WS, *Poems,* 396). Stevens converts the "strong persons who look at themselves as fact" (Em, 187–88) into fiction where they become the major men whose lives and works are one. From "The hum of thoughts evaded in the mind" (WS, *Poems,* 388; GS, *Phil,* 382), Stevens generates a poem for the life Santayana called spiritual since it is one lived "before the convent," "in the presence of the ideal." But the man becomes a poem only because, unlike Santayana's own Icarian metaphysician in his poem "On the Death of a Metaphysician," he spent his life studying, reading, writing comparative temperaments, historical, contemporary, autobiographical: "There are lives, nevertheless, which exist by the deliberate choice of those that live them. To use a single illustration: it may be assumed that the life of Professor Santayana is a life in which the function of the imagination has had a function similar to its function in any deliberate work of art or letters" (WS, *Essays,* 147–48).

It is the poet's needy imagination that levitates for us Santayana's body and scene from its chosen poverty of the "veritable small" to the "radiant and productive atmosphere" of the "illumined large" so that, as each of us "Beholds himself" in him (WS, *Essays,* 62; *Poems,* 508–9), we feel we might "ourselves form the margin of some more really central self" (WJ, *Plur,* 131; cf. WS, *Essays,* 62). As a "commiserable" man, like Emerson's "impressionable" man, Santayana stands with us in "the drag of temperament and race" to show us how to "take sides with the Deity who secures universal benefit by his pain" (Em, 350–51). The poet avoids idolatry of the life on one side and insufficient identification with it on the other by, in the mode of his master, recasting all ideals into the virtual mode, movingly evidenced by the domination of the final "realized" of the poem by "as if." And if temperament's poverty is there with spirit, so is its temptation. Stevens might very well see the philosopher behind the poet in this comment, since Santayana turned to Rome for relief from the anxiety of animal faith and the faith of American democratic Protestantism: "the truth about the poet in a time of disbelief is not that he must turn evangelist. After all, he shares the disbelief of his times. He does not turn to Paris or Rome for relief from the monotony of reality" (WS, *Opus,* 264). If his body is seeking only relief, not belief, the philosopher's mind had always promised us it would keep spirit busy catching "The eye of a vagabond in metaphor" sent out by the poet's hungry intuition (WS, *Poems,* 397). The convent could help Santayana to a "better focussed, more chastened, and more profound attention" to draw out life's venom. But that attention comes upon disinterested essences from the interested world of perceived appearances, chosen by the "bent of the animal that elicits the vision of them from his own soul and its adventures," a temperament able only in momentary fantasy to think itself lifted out of that context (GS, *Phil,* 424, 396).

Stevens's poem provisionally raises the room and body of Santayana into a transparent medium that is as free as possible from our "infusion[s] of reverie" and from the barbarism of "perpetual vagrancy" to which we are prone (GS, *Phil,* 424; *Interp,* 124). It lets us feel the sensation of incremental coaxing out by characteristic hyperqualifications, of essence by intuition, the mind's longed for meeting with "The vivid thing in the air that never changes, / Though the air change" (WS, *Poems,* 238). The threshold, as climactic location, felt transition, reminds us that we are, even at the end, only in "the immensest theatre" that joins, as logic cannot, two worlds, one of temperamentally anxious animal faith in which our incipient major man is, like us, "most penitent," and one of its fictive expansion that makes the "visible a little hard / To see" (WS, *Poems,* 311), in which we can almost feel, through our Major Man, impenitent. The poetry of virtual action that "disentangle(s)" us from "sleek ensolacings," from "false engagements of the mind" (WS, *Poems,* 317, 322), includes, like gossip, "all imaginative moral life" (GS, *Rel,* 43). It rises to the innocence of the most "earnest considerations" and "concentration" where the "eye of spirit sees the visible in its true setting of the invisible" (GS, *Phil,* 469). By this swelling, entrepreneured by the "as if" that first lifts us in line 8 to imagine "The human end in the spirit's greatest reach," the poem, through "engenderings of sense" (WS, *Poems,* 527) engenders truths upon the world (WJ, *Prag,* 123).

Our Major Man, "rugged roy" (WS, *Poems,* 302), born of our racial temperament, but not domesticated by its pathos, can momentarily chasten us out of "urgency and venom" (GS, *Phil,* 397) by his savage or primitive integrity as Emersonian Fact. As a god might be, Santayana, in the poem, is a character "beyond / Reality, composed thereof" (WS, *Poems,* 335). But, "commiserable," he does not commiserate like the old god of pity, or he would not be able to make us, who imagine him, work to make ourselves larger. When Stevens's descending angel, whom we *enjoy* (WS, *Poems,* 404–5), "comes down" upon us "clothed in a thousand phenomena" (GS, *Phil,* 585), he stirs us from impressionistic passivity to imaginative activity by closing out the dualism that divorces appearance from essence. And when our gods rise out of our poverty, "impatient for the grandeur" that they "need," they must, moving from our moody conditioning to supreme fiction, speak ahead of us into the Jamesian prospective, drawing us to a provisional perch from which "it is the human that is the alien" (WS, *Poems,* 328). Santayana's "god in the house," whose speech is demanded by human "poverty's speech," is cool to the need that calls on it for pity (WS, *Poems,* 327–28). The freeing of imaginative depth from the shallows of tautological pity comes with the full acknowledgment that "the oracles of spirit all have to be discounted" by seekers of Truth; "they are uttered in a cave" (GS, *Sense*, 8).

Such a cold drawing on and out as deep calls unto deep, our voice's origin becoming "less ours," though never free from its inspirited beginnings blown forth by "an afflatus of ruin," is "no facile exercise" (WS, *Poems*, 398); it works persistently toward "a creation of the imagination at its utmost" (WS, *Opus*, 266). Like spirit, the poem itself is busy turning things into objects of belief as it achieves a "moral actuality," and, like spirit, the poem is "actualised in actualising something else, an image or a feeling or an intent or a belief" (GS, *Phil*, 447). Its "as if" suspends, provisionally, Santayana's old body and his poor room, as it makes them a little hard to see, in a transparent building-out toward "total grandeur of a total edifice," the house chosen by an "inquisitor of structures," where presence and force seem one (WS, *Poems*, 436–37). We rise almost out of our "celestial pantomime" into a "celestial possible" where we experience "things" not "transformed," though "we are shaken by them as if they were" (WS, *Poems*, 243, 509, 399). The "sense of omnipotence" is "soon dispelled," the hero of the poem reminds us, "by recurring conflicts with hostile forces," but "the momentary illusion of that realized good has left us with the perennial knowledge of good as an ideal" (GS, *Interp*, 33).

The compounding of "the imagination's Latin with / The lingua franca et jocundissima" (WS, *Poems*, 397) has forced Rome to the "spirit's greatest reach," not into the old Beyond, but stopped at the stage's apron: "the extreme of the known in the presence of the extreme / Of the unknown." The "illumined large" rises out of the "luminous traversing" between temper and spirit, as the candle, evading the sight, becomes "the highest candle," but in Plato's cave (WS, *Poems*, 30, 524). We are all, for a moment, moved by the "parental magnitude" of the poem; we are collected in a "central mind" by the "intensest rendezvous" of Santayana with his Interior Paramour, of Stevens with his Santayana (WS, *Poems*, 524). But the "as if" that qualifies "two parallels" at the beginning of the poem warns us against both the mystic escapism of merging and a ritualized realization, keeping "that ideal vanishing point" of all truths engendered and acknowledged by need (WJ, *Prag*, 106–7; cf. GS, *Phil*, 525; GS, *Interp*, 163). Our swelling scene of "size and solitude" (WS, *Poems*, 443) must not be cut by virtue nor curtailed by the major lure to resignation: "What better than to blow out the candle and to bed" (GS, *Phil*, 418).

If Emerson claimed that "Temperament shuts . . . us in a prison of glass which we cannot see" (Em, 258), he also gave his poets, through their representative philosophers, the power to raise a god out of that cell, into a world "revolving" only "in crystal" (WS, *Poems*, 407). The "impossible possible philosophers' man" becomes our "central man" and makes our "globe, responsive / As a mirror with a voice" as he, "the man of glass," "in a million diamonds sums us up" (WS, *Poems,* 250). The transparence we seek to move into, "To face the weather and be unable to tell / How much of it was light and how much thought" (WS, *Poems,* 257), begins in the temperament "often untutored and seemingly incapable of being tutored, insensible to custom and law, marginal, grotesque" (WS, *Opus,* 253). Its persistent pestering of spirit led Emerson to confess: "I am Defeated all the time; yet to Victory am I born" (Em, 209). In the face of this recognition, Santayana links the sense of defeat to imagination's "bereavements": "a complete mastery of existence achieved at one moment gives no warrant that it will be sustained or achieved again at the next."[38] The modern imagination is not free to yield itself to Plato's "gorgeous nonsense" (WS, *Essays,* 4), but its poetry, listening intently to temperament's gossip with spirit, has the expressive power to say: "Life's nonsense pierces us with strange relation" (WS, *Poems,* 383). The courage to return us to this sense of candor is, at least, "the heroic effort to live *expressed* as victory" (WS, *Poems,* 446). The poet, a man "disposed to be strongly influenced by his imagination, which he believes, for a time, to be true, expressed in terms of his emotions, or . . . in terms of his own personality" (WS, *Essays,* 54), brings "poetic truth" to a provisional "agreement with reality." By this effort, James's confluent universe becomes the "fluent mundo" of Montaigne's gay and sociable wisdom (WS, *Poems,* 407).

---

38. George Santayana, *Reason in Art,* 136. Also see Santayana's definition of spiritual life in "Apologia Pro Mente Sua," 569.

3

THE IMAGINATION OF MORALITY

James, Conrad, and the
Lessons of the French Masters

Charles de Bernard's talent is great—very great, greater than the impression it leaves; and the reason why this clever man remains so persistently second-rate is, to my sense, because he had no morality. By this of course I do not mean that he did not choose to write didactic tales, winding up with a goodly lecture, and a distribution of prizes and punishments. I mean that he had no moral emotion, no preference, no instincts—no moral imagination, in a word.

Henry James

"You're *blasé,* but you're not enlightened. You're familiar with everything, but conscious really of nothing. What I mean is that you've no imagination."
Milly to Lord Mark, *The Wings of the Dove*

The history of Henry James's adventure among the French literary practitioners of his time has been reviewed, but not its heroism.[1] James enlisted a language and tactic of battle, in and out of the novel, to release into rich relations with psychology, spirit, and imagination the morality Flaubert had confined in provincial philistinism. The battlefield on which he had to fight the admired enemy was the scorched earth of Flaubert's irony, all the "shouted watchwords" exposed as the empty rhetoric of an exhausted ideal-

---

1. See, for example, Leon Edel, *The Life of Henry James;* Vivien Jones, *Henry James the Critic;* and Philip Grover, *Henry James and the French Novel.* See also Adeline R. Tintner, *The Cosmopolitan World of Henry James: An Intertextual Study,* and Edwin Sill Fussell, *The French Side of Henry James.*

ism.[2] James would have agreed with D. H. Lawrence that Flaubert was a hero of this necessary demolition, yet he viewed his martyred mission as a faithless fight, a "policy," in fact, "of flight." He sent his characters through the gates to perish while he stood outside, "upright as a sentinel."[3]

Well, insists James, "the shining arms were meant to carry further." Flaubert was right: we cannot return to Balzac's Parisian battlefield where talented dandies and geniuses of subversion ambitiously stormed the social hierarchy. Nevertheless, James advised Flaubert's successors to "go back to Balzac" to catch the courage with which he fought passionately at the side of his soldiers of society, letting them fight even his commands, each after his or her fashion; his genius was their genius.[4]

In characterizing his mission, Henry James made use of his brother's definition of the active and bold moral life as an acknowledgment that we are ourselves the heroes and heroines of our own "temperamental and partial stories" and have a willingness to put them into competition with the partial stories of others. And in the fierce collisions and cooperations of the potentially closed forms and diction of melodrama, Christian allegory, fairy tales, morality is measured by the intensity, quality, generosity of demands and concessions made in the negotiations between self-idealizations. James promises us adventure and trouble from the beginning of *The Wings of the Dove* when he has his Kate add to her announcement to Densher ("I shall try for everything. That . . . is how I see myself") these ominous words: "and how I see you quite as much." In imitation of life, to be morally persuasive, the melodrama of trial and temptation would have to suffer the impurity of participation by an author's "individual strong temperament," passionate in its aesthetic attractions and judgments, negotiating the liberty of his characters.[5] Balzac knew better and more gladly that "there is no such thing in the world as adventure pure and simple; there is only mine and yours, and his and hers," and he knew, as well, that if this was an invitation to domination, it was also the means of "robustly" enjoying "the sense of another explored, assumed, assimilated identity," freely

---

2. Joseph Conrad, "Henry James: An Appreciation," in *Joseph Conrad on Fiction,* 85; henceforth cited as JC, *Fic.*

3. Lawrence, "Review on Georgian Poetry 1911–1912," in *Phoenix,* 304; Gustave Flaubert (henceforth cited as GF) to Louise Colet, September 4, 1852, in *Selected Letters of Gustave Flaubert* (henceforth cited as *Sel*), 141. Henry James (henceforth cited as HJ), "Introduction to *Madame Bovary*" (henceforth cited as "Bov"), in *Literary Criticism* (henceforth cited as *Crit*), 2:337; "Correspondance de Gustave Flaubert" (henceforth cited as "deFL"), *Crit,* 2:314.

4. HJ, "deFl," *Crit,* 2:314; HJ, "The Present Literary Situation in France" (henceforth cited as "France"), *Crit,* 1:121; Hippolyte Taine, *Balzac: A Critical Study,* 171.

5. WJ, *Prag,* 11, 24, 71; *Will,* 150. HJ, "The Lesson of Balzac" (henceforth cited as "Balz"), *Crit,* 2:125, 132, 135; *The Wings of the Dove* (henceforth cited as *Dove*), 102.

contending with authorial plans. No one was more aware of how thoroughly temperament could ruin principle than Flaubert, who was hardly thrilled with the "adventure" of being himself. That is why he let his bourgeois characters die from the stupidity of their sentiments or live in the stupidity of their opinions. His martyrdom to "the plastic idea" demanded a withdrawal from his cast of his moral interest, of the dignity and freedom of competing compositions he leveled by a strong temperament protected from participation by parody and by a battlefield not worth fighting on. Flaubert appropriated for himself the privilege of justice, revenge, and refuge.[6]

In the wake of this powerful program of purification, James was driven to a heroic defense of Balzac's legacy of a medium bristling with the active morality of contending ambitions. As he makes obvious in his comments on writers like Maupassant, who "came into the literary world . . . under the protection of the great Flaubert," and in countless reviews and essays, he, himself, was parrying French disciples on the "Battle-field of . . . inevitable contrasts and competitors," in a common cause, out of his own psychological and cultural case, so remarkably correlative, to promote an allied Anglo-American temperamental context for the novel of deep and subtle moral consciousness and expression against that furiously conditioned by Flaubert's irony. Since Conrad's temper, shadowed by that of his fearless father, needed, as well, the prerogative of transferring to the act of seeing and telling in the novel the same value and valor formerly invested in "the clash of arms and sound of trumpets," the same interest as "the surprise of a caravan or the identification of a pirate," "the fiercest excitements of a romance *de cape et d'epéé*," thoroughly debased by the cheap fantasies of Madame Bovary, he eagerly saw James, the "historian of fine consciences," as a hero of "rescue work carried out in darkness against cross gusts of wind."

French boldness in narrating sexual and sentimental educations made art seem more worldly action than aesthetic contemplation. But, while deeply impressed by Flaubert's example and checked by his assault on the watchwords of idealism, Conrad could assign courage a new climax, the "supreme energy of an act of renunciation," because James draped "the robe of spiritual honour about the drooping form of a victor in a barren strife. And the honour is always well won." If he leaves his soldiers on the battlefield, he leaves them with a free moral imagination backed by their fearless recorder of all the "*péripéties* of the contest and the feeling of the combatants" (JC, *Fic,* 85, 87, 84). If his penetration into the scene cannot be as spontaneous and innocent as that of Balzac, his tender watching assures to those he loves the power of seeing. As a critic, James enacts his contest with the

6. HJ, "Bov," *Crit,* 2:313, 337; GF to George Sand, December 18–19, 1867, in *The Letters of Gustave Flaubert, 1857–1880* (henceforth cited as *Ltrs*), 113.

contemporary French claims he tests in his novels, and, by recording all the feelings of his combatants, he fights Taine for the soul of English moralism and Flaubert for the imagination of morality. He knows that, after Flaubert, in the final words of his Kate Croy, "we shall never be again as we were." But he wants the satisfaction of knowing that he will be one whom the great French master "gazing" on the "ocean of art" will see navigating or doing battle."[7]

We cannot ignore, under James's clear appointment of Flaubert as indisputable maker and master of the modern idiom, muffled tones of anger, fear, anxiety that curl into incipient condescension. The American novelist early assented to the historical imperative for a correction of Sand's romance of nobility that ran over the resistance of actuality. He knew Flaubert was right to insist that the new novelist could no longer sing the "simple tunes" of the sentimental idealist; a syntax of ironic deflation needed to punish a moribund "mercy, humanitarianism, . . . ideal" that had "played us sufficiently false to make us try Righteousness and Science."[8] Yet he seems almost tender to the "sentimental authority" of George Sand's generosity in the face of her demotion to patroness of a stale appeal to the sublime and the beautiful. He is moved by this fate: "During the last half of her career, her books went out of fashion among the new literary generation. 'Realism' had been invented, or rather propagated; and in light of 'Madame Bovary' her own facile fictions began to be regarded as the work of a sort of superior Mrs. Radcliffe. She was antiquated; she belonged to the infancy of art."[9]

And he seems squeamish in anticipation of a vulgar adoption of the new tone by the avant-garde after hearing Paul Bourget's 1877 lecture on Flaubert at conservative Oxford.[10] Even in a late essay, when he spoke for all the great modern novelists, he felt impelled to add a severe qualification. If "we practise our industry . . . at relatively little cost just *because* poor Flaubert, producing the most expensive fictions ever written, so handsomely paid for it," we need to remember, as well, that he was "the most conspicuous of the faithless" (HJ, "Bov," *Crit,* 2:332; "deFl," *Crit,* 2:313).

Behind the demurrals is the devotion of James to the great progenitor of the new realists, Balzac, whom Flaubert had consigned to the "infancy of art." At Flaubert's Sunday cenacle in Paris, James felt drawn to the delicate Turgenev for the gentle pathos of his depiction of antiquated "senti-

7. HJ, "Preface to *The Wings of the Dove*" (henceforth cited as "Wings"), *Crit,* 2:1303; GF to Louise Colet, October 7, 1846, *Sel,* 85.
8. GF to Louise Colet, July 15, 1853, and George Sand, October 7, 1871, *Ltrs,* 157, 183.
9. HJ, "Letter from Paris: George Sand" (1876), *Crit,* 2:707; "George Sand" (1877) (henceforth cited as "Sand"), *Crit,* 2:721.
10. Edel, *James,* 4:184–85.

ment and ideal," but he reserved his deepest devotion for the coarse gargantuan father of the *Comédie humaine*. He did not protest Flaubert's distaste for Balzac's inflated style, his shabby tricks. But we are still a bit surprised by the single-minded nature of the love and respect the un-Balzacian James felt for the novelist he could criticize without guilt and apology.[11] The motive belongs at the center of the history of the American novelist's personal and national temperamental needs and faiths. The fussy historian of moral discriminations and fine conscience was captivated by the courage of Balzac's passionate participation in the genius of his characters and their temptations. Even if he was, by this investment, often an unsure moralist, he always "fought out his case," with his characters, "on the spot." Flaubert, on the other hand, became a "potent moralist" by his "policy of flight" from the caged medium in which his characters struggle.[12] James continually asked himself why the novelist who carelessly adulterated his moral with aesthetic judgment was the one who could give him the means and manner by which to compass a wider dimension for English moralism, to some extent justly under Taine's attack for caring more about the desire to be good than that to write passionately, well, and beyond convention.

Though, in a tone of disgust, Flaubert lumped Taine with the overschooled materialists of naturalism, he must have known Sainte-Beuve had anticipated his connections with the anatomist of race, moment, and milieu. If Taine preferred to target a narrow and puritanical English moralism that forced even great hypocrites like Pecksniff to imitate gospel goodness, Flaubert aimed at the memorized morality of provincial French tempers ruined by the slogans of Romantic revolutions and novels. Both prepared the way for Nietzsche's complaint that the English didn't even realize that morality had become a problem.[13] Taine located the French genius in the sublime

11. Harry Levin has called James "probably the least Balzacian of novelists" (*The Gates of Horn: A Study of Five French Realists*, 166). This judgment of temper must be balanced by the recognition of Adeline R. Tintner in *The Book World of Henry James*, 245, that Balzac was for James the "greatest multiple source for literary models," as earlier noted by Peter Brooks in his comparison of hypersignificant textures, the relations between the morality and melodrama of postsacral stage and novel, in *The Melodramatic Imagination: Balzac, Henry James, Melodrama, and the Mode of Excess*. See further discussion of Brooks's thesis in Ruth Newton and Naomi Lebowitz, *Dickens, Manzoni, Zola, and James: The Impossible Romance*. In his famous essay "Criticism and Fiction," W. D. Howells, devoted to Balzac the realist, patronized his artistic "infancy" by claiming the French novelist did not have the advantage of writing after Balzac.

12. HJ, "Bov," *Crit*, 2:326, 337; see also "Charles de Bernard and Gustave Flaubert: The Minor Novelists" (henceforth cited as "Bern"), *Crit*, 2:169.

13. HJ, "Guy de Maupassant" (henceforth cited as "Maup"), *Crit*, 2:552; "Pierre Loti" (henceforth cited as "Loti"), *Crit*, 2:483. (The last line of Sainte-Beuve's famous essay on *Madame Bovary* [1857] is this apostrophe: "Anatomists and physiologists. I find you

where society and law could be transgressed in the name of a higher moral-ity; Flaubert, on the other hand, protested the degradation of that sublime in a philistine world by summing up its formulas from the mouth of a trivial villain, Rodolphe, whose seductive quarrels with duty climaxed in reductive clichés of Sandian idealism. He, himself, gives us the terms by which to identify his task with that of Taine: "concern with morality makes every work of the imagination false and stupid. . . . I am becoming quite a critic. The novel I am writing sharpens this faculty, for it is essentially a work of criticism, or rather of anatomy." Taine, as well, is only too happy to blur the line between literature and criticism: "In France, criticism has a freer gait; it is less subordinate to morality and more akin to art."[14]

The example of Flaubert, Taine, and the naturalists had convinced James that morality *should* have problems in the English and American novel, but it also gave him the impetus to fight on all fronts, critical and creative, for its right to live in a discriminating and dramatic medium in the com-pany of an intelligent imagination. Politely reproaching the French for neglect and misreading of English fiction, behind a screen of universalism, he sets himself up as a competitor to Taine in order to counterattack the French scorn of English moralism: "He remains an interpreter of the English mind to the mind of another race; and only remotely, therefore—only by allowance and assistance,—an interpreter of the English mind to itself. A greater fault than any of his special errors of judgment is a certain re-duced, contracted, and limited air in the whole field. He has made his subject as definite as his method." James calls the "complex fate of the American" a fight against a "superstitious valuation of Europe," mani-fested in his characters as a persistent under- or overreading, with grave consequences, of national traits and types. Taine pushes a national story that is quite insensitive to the "English genius for psychological observa-tion," devoted not to theory but to character and to its "mysteries and secrets of conscience." His tough and lively critical tone is deaf to the "indefinable quality of spiritual initiation which is the tardy consummate fruit of a wasteful, purposeless, passionate sympathy."[15]

If, withal, he can still read Balzac well in his *History of English Litera-ture,* he reads him against the English, alternately as an idealist and as a

---

everywhere.") GF to George Sand, circa December 31, 1875, *Ltrs,* 227. Hippolyte Taine, *The History of English Literature,* 4:149; henceforth cited as Taine, *Hist.* GF to Turgenev, late 1877, and Mme des Genettes, March 3, 1877, *Ltrs,* 242, and commentary, 242; Friedrich Nietzsche, "Expeditions of an Untimely Man," 70.

14. Taine, *Hist,* 4:143–4, 235; GF to Louise Colet, January 2, 1854, *Sel,* 167.

15. HJ, "Review of Taine's *History of English Literature*" (henceforth cited as "Tain"), *Crit,* 2:843; "Maup," *Crit,* 2:549–50; to Charles Eliot Norton, February 1872, *Henry James: Selected Letters* (henceforth cited as *Ltrs*), 93; "Review of *Notes sur l'Angleterre,*" *Crit,* 2:839.

materialist. This stirs James to confiscate his crucial identification of Balzac's patrimony: "'Balzac aime sa Valérie,' says Taine . . . speaking of the way in which the awful little Madame Marneffe . . . is drawn, and of the long rope, for her acting herself out, that her creator's participation in her reality assures her. He has been contrasting her, as it happens, with Thackeray's Becky Sharp or rather with Thackeray's attitude toward Becky, and the marked jealousy of her freedom that Thackeray exhibits from the first." If, James suggests, this participation is the source of Balzac's most powerful pictures, it is also the place of his best morality. Here, not in his moral sops to the reader, is an agency available to Anglo-American fiction. If Taine could use Balzac to criticize the Protestant moralism of a novel fearful of passionate transgressions, James could use him to help recover for it a larger range of relations, thickening the middle ground between idealism and materialism where "morals and aesthetics move in concert." We can go back to Balzac because he cares so much about character, and that is the source of the superiority of English novelists over French naturalists:

> It may fairly be said that the French *parti-pris* not only turns too persistent a back on those quarters of life in which character does play, but also—and with still less justice—tends to pervert and minimize the idea of "passion." Passion still abides with us, though its wings have undoubtedly been clipped; the possibility of it is, in the vulgar phrase, all over the place. But it lives a great variety of life, burns with other flames and throbs with other obsessions than the sole sexual. In some of these connections it absolutely *becomes* character; whereas character, on the contrary, encounters in the sexual the particular air, the special erotic fog, that most muffles and dampens it.[16]

This might be a fine anticipatory commentary on the atmosphere of *The Wings of the Dove,* and it gives us evidence of how persistently James worked out his critical competitions with the French in his own novels. The isolation of the sexual subject in the naturalists and in writers like Gabriele D'Annunzio and Matilde Serao from all the "finer possible combinations" and relations with spirit and psychology is a more severe constriction of the moral imagination than ever practiced by English moralism shy, like the American James, himself, of the sexual passions. That James finds these ramifying and generous relations in Balzac, that these relations mark him as a moralist of the imagination, is clear when he speaks of lesser talents:

> I like [Alphonse Daudet] . . . best of all the novelists who have not the greater imagination, the imagination of the moralist. . . . To stir the reader's moral

16. HJ, "Balz," *Crit,* 2:131. See also Conrad's use of the term *love* in a criticism of Thackeray: "A Glance at Two Books," JC, *Fic,* 73. HJ, "The Novels of George Eliot" (henceforth cited as "Eliot"), *Crit,* 1:933; "France," *Crit,* 1:121.

nature, and to write with truth and eloquence the moral history of superior men and women demand more freedom and generosity of mind than M. Feuillet seems to possess. Like those of most of the best French romancers, his works wear morally, to American eyes, a decidedly thin and superficial look. Men and women, in our conception, are deeper, more substantial, more self-directing; they have if not more virtue, at least more conscience; and when conscience comes into the game human history ceases to be a perfectly simple tale.[17]

This emphasis accounts, doubtlessly, for the shadow of scorn in James's judgment that *Madame Bovary* is the most "pointed" and "told" of stories, and not *immoral,* but as moral as a Sunday school lesson. To add insult to injury, he had earlier made poor Flaubert share a review with Charles Bernard, who is second-rate precisely because he "had no moral emotion, no preference, no instincts—no moral imagination," and with Feuillet a charge of offering to his heroine too small a quantity and quality of possible relations.[18] Persuasive arguments connecting Balzac and James by their relations to the theater of melodrama and symbolism have been developed by Peter Brooks and William W. Stowe.[19] For the common shift of moral emphasis to the participation of author in character, no negative example could be more valuable than the theater of Dumas fils. His moralizing in-spires this boutade James could have launched against Taine: "Whereas we like to be good the French like to be better." Dumas fils is entirely out of the range of Balzac's genius, which gives "the little invisible push that, even when shyly and awkwardly administered, makes the puppet, in spite of the string, walk off by himself and quite 'cut,' if the mood take him, that distant relation to his creator."[20]

However effectively Taine uses Balzac to clinch the French case against English moralism, James fights him on the spot for the great legacy and, in this way, appropriates for English criticism a boldness readers like Arnold Bennett, no great admirer of the American novelist, found only in Sainte-Beuve and Taine. The French critic has Balzac, rather than Flaubert, hold the hands of science and art over the head of Sunday moralism in a victory clasp: "When we have come to the end of Balzac's *Le Père Goriot,* our heart is pained by the tortures of that anguish; but the astonishing inventive-

17. HJ, "Gabriele D'Annunzio," *Crit,* 2:943; "Alphonse Daudet" (1897) (henceforth cited as "Daud"), *Crit,* 2:256; "Octave Feuillet" (henceforth cited as "Feu"), *Crit,* 2:285. The comparison to Feuillet would have been particularly galling to Flaubert, who scorned Feuillet's art.

18. HJ, "Bov," *Crit,* 2:323; "Bern," *Crit,* 2:166; "Bov," *Crit,* 2:328; see also "Preface to *The Portrait of a Lady*" (henceforth cited as "Lady"), *Crit,* 2:1072.

19. Brooks, *The Melodramatic Imagination,* and Stowe, *Balzac, James, and the Realistic Novel.*

20. HJ, "Dumas the Younger," in *The Scenic Art: Notes on Acting and the Drama, 1872–1901,* 269, 275.

ness . . . the abundance of general ideas, the force of analysis, transport us
into the world of science, and our painful sympathy is calmed by the specta-
cle of this physiology of the heart. Dickens never calms our sympathy."
What Taine is trying to separate is the logic of Balzac's passion and psychology from the instinct of English puritanism. Because Balzac's lovers
could be immoral and interesting, he can say to the English novelist: "You
may console yourself with the thought that you are moral. Your lovers will
be uninteresting." After Flaubert, whose lovers are drawn against those of
Balzac as immoral and uninteresting, James will be able to put on the
scene lovers like Kate Croy and Merton Densher who are, only to the
degree they are responsive to a rich amalgam of conscience and consciousness, immoral and interesting. The subtleties of these adjustments depend
upon James's promotion to moral use of Taine's measure: Balzac's generosity of participation. He recognizes in it a spiritual order of knowing, first
by loving, for that is what gives characters the capacity, fatally missing in
Adam Bede, "to be tempted."[21] That way of knowing stirs, as well, "the joy
of evocation" in the "imperfect reader" who is never "*totally* beguile[d]" by
mere form and style. The joy of composition, renounced by the anchoritic
Flaubert who leaves art "unconsoled, . . . unhumorous . . . unsociable," derives from the Balzacian delight in the liberty of his characters, "in their
communicated and exhibited movement, in their standing on their feet and
going of themselves." James names this sympathy that makes aesthetic
investment moral, assuring liberty to characters, "saturation" (HJ, "Bov,"
Crit, 2:340; "deFl," *Crit,* 2:298; "Balz," *Crit,* 2:133, 131–32).

He well recognized that Balzac's intensity of aesthetic delight in national
and racial stereotype could free a Jewish collector in *Cousin Pons* from the
condescension and sentimentality of George Eliot's morally earnest depiction of Jews in *Daniel Deronda.* The sign of saturation is, paradoxically, the
spontaneous burst of mutual cartooning, apparently out of reach of Balzac's control: "You are much too Marneffe altogether, Monsieur Marneffe!"
said the Baron. "You are much too Hulot altogether, Monsieur Hulot!" The
direct explosion, as against Flaubert's indirect summations, testifies to
Balzac's willingness to consign irony to other mouths, to the intensity of his
penetration into his scene and society, and gives us the sense that he pays,
body and soul, for his knowledge, a knowledge betraying inordinate interest in socializing his self-idealizing story. The creator as lover is necessarily
an amateur, willing to evoke the illusion of a mutual contamination of life
and art for the sake of multiplying the finer possibilities of mutual complic-

21. Arnold Bennett, "English Literary Criticism," in *Books and Persons: Being Comments on a Past Epoch: 1908–1911,* 267–70; Taine, *Hist,* 4:135, 144; HJ, "Eliot," *Crit,*
1:923.

ity, alibi, rationalization, and temptation. When James, after compliment-
ing the thoroughness of Flaubert's pictorial rendering in *Madame Bovary*,
snaps, "One can hardly congratulate him on his knowledge," we can read
"on his way of knowing," to condescend and confine. And, of course, this is a
response registered obsessively in James's novels, which share the evaluative diction of his criticism. The adjectives of professional completeness and
calculation that serve to depict and diminish Flaubert circle around Madame Merle, Osmond, and Kate.[22]

Using his favorite metaphor of international complexity, James speaks of
Balzac's anti-Flaubertian willingness to enter "the extraordinary number
and length of his radiating and ramifying corridors—the labyrinth in which
he finally lost himself," for that is where he gains his soul. This generous
and kenotic vulnerability, praised for its access to the politics of history by
readers as disparate as James, Proust, Lukács, and Sartre, is, in Flaubert's
eyes, Balzac's romance of narrative innocence.[23] For James, it generates
the romance of social complexity, the labyrinth that lures the naked clue of
Emersonian moral passion and teases out the smugness of English moralism into a compromised atmosphere of imaginative waste. It is easy to
forget that this blurring and expansion of morality by mystery is what
earned James entry into F. R. Leavis's Great Tradition, since, from the
contemporary perspective in which political and ontological discourse have
entirely repressed the moral (Paris, with the help of psychology and phe-
nomenology, having finally triumphed), that tradition appears insufferably
elitist and conservative. Balzac helped James to turn to fiction's account
the American pragmatism of his brother, which boasted of recovering the
"vague" for philosophy in order to keep system from suppressing temperament as a shaping agent of our moral life.

The constant premise of an energetic and active moral life in both philosophies and fictions was, for William and Henry James (and the James
character of high consciousness), the availability to the state of becoming
dupe of one's own medium and momentum. In the preface to *The Wings of
the Dove*, Henry asks, for them together: "some acute mind ought surely to
have worked out by this time the 'law' of the degree in which the artist's
energy fairly depends on his fallibility. How much and how often, and in
what connections and with what almost infinite variety, must he be a dupe,

22. Balzac, *Cousin Bette*, 273, 277. HJ, "Balz," *Crit*, 2:130; "Bern," *Crit*, 2:171. My
student Andrew Mozina helped me to see how pervasive this correspondence is.
23. HJ, "Balz," *Crit*, 2:127; GF to Edmond de Goncourt, December 31, 1876, *Ltrs*, 237.
Alain Robbe-Grillet, in the line of Flaubert and Brecht, speaks for modern minimalists
when he casts suspicion on the "myths" of referentiality and depth as a symptom of the
desire to dominate the world. We cannot go back to Balzac, whose surfaces lured us to the
hidden secrets of life and power. "A Future for the Novel," in *For a New Novel: Essays on
Fiction*, 23–24.

that of his prime object, to be at all measurably a master, that of his actual substitute for it—or in other words at all appreciably to exist."[24] *Because* Balzac had "no natural sense of morality" in the great scenes of temptation in which he lost himself, *because* he gives us an "aesthetic judgment" where we expect a moral one, and *because* he insists on granting his bourgeois reader the grace of overthorough transitions he believes adequate to account for everything that happens, he achieves a depth of illusion that sinks him "up to his chin" in the trials of the moral life, not, "as the weak and timid in this line do, only up to his ankles or his knees."[25] James borrowed this image from his own climactic movement in *The Wings of the Dove* in which the spiritual beauty of Milly rolls out on a tide that floats Densher "up to his chin" in a new medium. The imagery of immersion is set against the principle of Flaubert's "impersonality" standing "sentinel" at the door of depth he should have entered: "This would have floated him on a deeper tide; above all it would have calmed his nerves" (HJ, *Dove*, 334; "deFl," *Crit*, 2:314).

We need to remember that Taine had taken Dickens to task for not calming our sympathies by achieving the transparency of the sublime perspective. James implies Flaubert would have had a less anxious and exacerbated martyrdom of disequilibrium if he had taken his character through a more difficult moral medium since "it is somehow the business of a protagonist to prevent in his designer an excessive waste of faith" (HJ, "Bov," *Crit*, 2:327). The saturation that made Balzac his own "most perfect dupe" and gave him such aesthetic joy that it could serve as morality *in* the novel without Nietzsche's transvaluation was, to Flaubert, a terror. He so dreaded becoming the dupe of his characters' illusions, of those of his readers, that he excluded them by his martyrdom. Usually protected from the temptations of mediocrity by a pitiless syntax of blameless irony skewering the political pretensions of a character like Hussonnet, whose indirect claim not to be taken in any more rhetorically impales itself, Flaubert in his Romantic book is the celibate saint, standing in for St. Anthony against his readers ("Instead of St. Anthony . . . *I* am in my book; and I, rather than the reader, underwent the temptation"). He is cruelly anti-Romantic, when he gives to Madame Bovary's suffering only the outlet of her stupidity. A tendency to abuse irony, which James spotted even in Turgenev, revered for his moral interest in character, might be a sign of

24. HJ, "A Memoir of Ralph Waldo Emerson," *Crit*, 1:257; "Wings," *Crit*, 2:1294–95. And see the comments of Richard A. Hocks, *Henry James and Pragmatist Thought: A Study in the Relationship between the Philosophy of William James and the Literary Art of Henry James*, 76–80.

25. HJ, "Honoré de Balzac" (1875) (henceforth cited as "Hono"), *Crit*, 2:49; "Balz," *Crit*, 2:128.

this horror of the contamination of art by the life in love with a cheapened rhetoric of grace, humanitarianism, sentiment, and the ideal. It could be motivated by personal spites and tempers, the humiliating double desire to be good and to get vengeance, the Balzacian belief in the possible progress of private and national histories through the temptations they generate. Viewing a punishing and distancing realism as a mode of self-protection, a way of avoiding errors, and an agency of vengeance against all that would bring down the higher morality of Art, Flaubert makes himself into a sacrificial gladiator, into a religious saint scapegoated into salvation. As one of the "Christs of art," he might be able to cure the leprosy of Eugène Sue, suffering the same symptom as Balzac and Sand: "infancy of art." He might even, as a lesser martyr, his St. Antoine or Julien, almost embrace the leprous language of democratic Christian humanism and idealism, but only by parody, holding it to the level of sensation and stupidity, to gain his ascent against it.[26]

An effective cure for the incipient infection, the potential morality of sympathy, was to transfer it to the bodies of swine, where it could choke on the materialism of Homais's "philistine radicalism" (HJ, "Bern," *Crit,* 2:174) or Madame Bovary's sensational philistinism. His antidote to dupism is distance, but not the distance Henry and William James, with Nietzsche, see as necessary to the survival of a coolly viewed self-idealization. Flaubert, instead, withdraws from the moral expectations of sentimental readers and the moral stupidity of sentimental characters, since, unlike Balzac, he is not a novelist who loves his own vices.[27] His strategy is to starve the text's morality, reducing radically the range and subtlety of its psychological relations, its discriminations, its imaginations. "Would it ever occur to anyone," a reader asks, "to participate in any of the numerous conversations in *L'Education sentimentale?*" The attack is justified by the contemporary bourgeois practice that would put his niece in an educational "strait-jacket" and dream of god as "an oriental monarch surrounded by his court": "every piece of writing must have its moral significance, must teach a lesson, elementary or advanced; a sonnet must be given philosophical implications; a play must rap the knuckles of the royalty and a watercolor contribute to moral progress."[28]

26. HJ, "Hono," *Crit,* 2:47; GF, *Sentimental Education* (henceforth cited as *Sent*), 145; GF to his mother, December 15, 1850, Louise Colet, July 6, 1852, and June 2, 1854, Ernest Feydeau, first half of October 1859, and Louis Bouilhet, November 14, 1850, *Sel,* 112, 138, 167–68, 202, 108.

27. Nietzsche, *The Gay Science,* 133; Charles du Bos, "Flaubert," in *Approximations,* 172.

28. Quoted from J. Meier-Gräfe by M. M. Bakhtin, *Problems of Dostoevsky's Poetics,* 6; GF to his mother, November 14, 1850, Mme des Genettes, 1859 or 1860, and Louise Colet, September 18, 1846, *Sel,* 110, 19, 77.

How better to stop "moral progress" than by paralyzing moral action in the novel at the lazy level of memorization and recitation. This might accomplish what James imagined was the aim of Flaubert's martyrdom: revenge against and refuge from the mixed medium of life and art in which Balzac so willingly lived, getting *his* revenge by living well. In contrast to the energy of Balzac's symbiosis of spiritual waste, Flaubert's severe economy by separation is entropy: "the comparatively meager human consciousness—for we must come back to that in him—struggling with the absolutely large artistic; and the large artistic half wreaking itself on the meager human half and seeking a refuge from it, as well as a revenge against it, in something quite different" (HJ, "Bov," *Crit,* 2:336–37). A novel like *Salammbo* gains license for the large artistic consciousness to entertain the guiltless picturesque of "old cruelties and perversities" by featuring the absence of "a philosopher . . . who would be portrayed as giving a course in morals or as performing good actions—a gentleman in short who 'feels as we do.'"[29]

The most damaging strategy practiced in the bourgeois novels is the collapsing of morality into sensation: "I want to write the moral history of the men of my generation—or, more accurately, the history of their *feelings.* It's a book about love, about passion; but passion such as can exist nowadays—that is to say, inactive." This demotion of active morality to affective fantasy virtually eliminates resistance of subject and subjects to "le mot juste," itself a precise protest against the absence of just action in a world that has already infected the blood of its surgeon who adopts the virtue of not acting in the world. A novelist could even be so little dupe as to imagine writing a book against Balzac's quantity, about nothing, making it easy for temperament to embrace fate: "how difficult it is to write something that has substance and at the same time *moves.*"[30]

The passion that had suffered post-Napoleonic degradation in the "bourgeois" novels of Balzac was decidedly not inactive. It met a morally and aesthetically vivid world in which to enact ambition before it could waste itself in fantasy. By draining values from the world, Flaubert inflates a life of paralyzing projections that can neither organize public history, educate suffering, nor enjoy the autonomy of its natural and artificial furnishings. While Balzac's houses energetically express character, Flaubert's only attract undeveloped sentiment; his Nature cuts off the active consolation of

29. HJ, "Bov," *Crit,* 2:340; GF to Sainte-Beuve, December 23–24, 1862, *Ltrs,* 45. This "absence" answers, as well, Sainte-Beuve's complaint that there were virtually no "good" characters in *Madame Bovary.*

30. GF to Mademoiselle Leroyer de Chantepie, October 6, 1864, Louise Colet, January 16, 1852, and Ernest Feydeau, November 24, 1857, *Sel,* 80, 127, 6. See also Michel Butor, *Improvisations sur Flaubert,* 32: In such an unworthy world, indolence could be virtue.

pathetic fallacy. And now, when French morality must be exposed as sensation, education in the novel can only be sentimental, in order to justify authorial escape from wasteful sympathies in an unworthy medium. Even a bourgeois novel could have its surface calmed into a moral picturesque, to quiet the tiring alternation of preaching and aesthetic seduction enjoyed by Balzac, who still hoped, both in and out of the novel, for the union of aesthetic beauty and social happiness that Flaubert thought impossible. To protest Flaubert's enervating distancing and promote Balzac's invigorating dupism, James resorts to the practice of indirect criticism through inferior artists. He economically recycles Taine's characterization of Prosper Mérimée's weak spots in which we conveniently find Flaubert's cherished terms of higher morality, "science" and "art": "For fear of being dupe, he *mistrusted* in life, in love, in science, in art; and he was *dupe of his mistrust.* One is always dupe of something." Daudet's charming picturesque at least risks warmth, while Flaubert's "cold picturesque" of passive aggression is that of his remote painter at Fontainebleau: "a kind of grand measured distance from his canvas—posed as if for a duel—to attack his subject with a brush 20 feet long."[31]

It is really on the battlefield of Balzac that James spars with Flaubert to rescue the grace of moral imagination as a respondent to the new justice. He sensed what we now, hyperconscious about the burden of the past and the anxiety of influence, see even more clearly, that Flaubert's penchant for fastidiousness and fantasy was motivated to creative energy and self-protection by a deliberate subversion of Balzacian strategies. Flaubert felt compelled to disperse the rich connections between things and characters and to collapse the dramatic play between materialism and idealism, justifying the move by this astute and squeamish reading of his own body: "I am convinced that the most raging material appetites express themselves unwittingly in outbursts of idealism, just as the most obscene carnal excesses are engendered by pure desire for the impossible, ethereal aspiration toward supreme bliss."[32] Balzac's innocent and joyous exploitation and exploration of those sumptuous relations serve to legitimate him as the enemy. Subvert the thrilling seriousness of the secret codes and initiations of tiered societies; disappoint the expected sequence of temptation, repetition, and moral, social, professional progress; collapse dramatic associations between syntax and discrimination of value in act and imagination; prevent spontaneous expression by indirect summation; make cold and abrupt the transitions between parts of sentences, paragraphs, chapters

31. GF to Louise Colet, August 21–22, 1853, *Sel,* 161. HJ, "Prosper Merimeé," *Crit,* 2:571; "Flaubert: *La Tentation de Saint Antoine*" (henceforth cited as "Tent"), *Crit,* 2:294; "Daud," *Crit,* 2:256.
32. GF to Mademoiselle Leroyer de Chantepie, February 18, 1859, *Ltrs,* 15–16.

since they are constant reminders of Balzac's special pleading. Stopping Balzacian momentum at all levels of syntax, plot, spirit, and power is both the psychological symptom and the political instrument of Flaubert's policy of refuge and revenge. The disciple converts the passionate and evil conspiracies that testify to moral hope and responsibility into stupidity that denies both. Only the generously intelligent dupe can convert moral and formal duplicity to dialectic.

Yet James realizes, with his fellow modern novelists, that Balzac could not be persuasively regained for a new age except through Flaubert's revolution. The license for Balzac's passionate interest in the temptations of his characters was his subscription to the conservative givens of governmental and domestic order as fixed principles. By scoring these values as political formulas, Flaubert took the novel into the age of Nietzsche: "The words 'religion' or 'Catholicism' on the one hand, 'progress,' 'brotherhood,' 'democracy' on the other, no longer satisfy the spiritual demands of our time. The brand-new dogma of equality, preached by Radicalism, is given the lie by experimental psychology and by history. I do not see how it is possible today to establish a new Principle, or to respect the old ones." A democratizing irony and syntax could at least level the perverted dogma of equality, stopping narrative progress and fraternity in their tracks. So imperious is Flaubert's revenge of counterleveling he bursts into his novel to sneer at the National Guard: "Despite their victory, equality—as if to punish its defenders and ridicule its enemies—asserted itself triumphantly: an equality of brute beasts."[33]

For the spiritual demands of the time to be educated and somehow fed from the scorched earth of false idealism, it was up to the pragmatists of passionate interest in the partial stories of their characters (for William and Henry James the very sign of moral seriousness) to negotiate a way back to Balzac through the pretense of Flaubert's disinterest in the complete stories of his characters. William James registers the transvaluating adjustment from a post-Darwinian perspective: "Our spirit, shut within the courtyard of sense-experience, is always saying to the intellect upon the tower: 'Watchman, tell us of the night, if it aught of promise bear,' and the intellect gives it then these terms of promise. Other than this practical significance, the words God, free-will, design, etc. have none. Yet dark tho they be in themselves, or intellectualistically taken, when we bear them into life's thicket with us the darkness *there* grows light about us."[34] Without the martyrdom of James's "poor Flaubert," extricating himself from the thicket by what Auerbach termed his style of "objective seriousness, seek-

---

33. HJ, "Balz," *Crit,* 2:131; GF to George Sand, December 20, 1875, *Sel,* 251; GF, *Sent,* 334.
34. WJ, *Prag,* 61.

ing to penetrate to the depths of the passions and entanglements of a human life, but without itself becoming moved," there would be no authentic roost for the modern painters of "tender imagination" necessarily reduced to "watching through the eyes of others."[35]

The syntactical harmony of the surface that deflates both moral and metaphorical discrimination in character and speech might serve Flaubert as a peculiar proxy for Platonism. The beauty of scornful form, clearly divided from its happiness and only occasionally broken by pathos, might make of the book "whose parts fit precisely, which is composed of rare elements, whose surface is polished, and which is a harmonious whole . . . an intrinsic Virtue, a kind of divine force, something as eternal as a principle." This kind of devotion could return the novelist to a classicism that makes all disagreeables evaporate and achieve, even, a version of the harmony, dreamed briefly through the immature mind of Madame Bovary, of virtue, sensuality, and duty. In the novel, the blank gaze of Flaubert's blind, begging, provincial Tiresias compels suppressed suffering to surface, destroying the dream of beauty and happiness, scaring the consciousness impotent to turn failure into the tragic sublime. His distant song carries the novelist upward, curing the work of all expectation of authorial grace. The tender imagination of the watcher is cut to secure the innocence of aesthetic convictions assuming the authority of moral principle by martyrdom in bourgeois history. James accepts the legitimacy of this ideal as the beginning of modernism, but only if it is read as the temperament Flaubert feared: "I am only too full of convictions. . . . But my ideal of Art demands that the artist reveal none of this and that he appear in his work no more than God in nature. The man is nothing, the work everything. . . . For me . . . it is a kind of perpetual sacrifice that I burn on the altar of good taste."[36] As with Kafka's Gregor, the body's disappearance assures the innocence of what is left behind, not the family, but the art that was so shamelessly prostituted by Balzac's saturation.

By this gesture, Flaubert forced the modern novel to make its unauthorized appeal to the language of idealism the very subject of the text. The novelist who, for James, perfected the most "pointed" and "told" of stories impels his Anglo-American successors to be such "votar[ies] of the way to do a thing that shall make it undergo most doing" as to make them vulnerable to the charge of fulfilling Flaubert's fantasy: to write novels about nothing.[37] With-

35. Erich Auerbach, "In the Hôtel de la Mole," in *Mimesis: The Representation of Reality in Western Literature,* 432; HJ, "Wings," *Crit,* 2:1303.

36. GF to George Sand, April 3, 1876, and after December 20, 1875, *Ltrs,* 252, 249–50.

37. HJ, "The New Novel" (henceforth cited as "New"), *Crit,* 1:147. H. G. Wells makes this charge against James in *Boon* (1915); for E. M. Forster against Conrad, see *Aspects of the Novel* (1927).

out Flaubert, could Conrad have released his terms of value from protective custody? Without Balzac, could he have given them the ring of "heroic truth," the right "accent" saving the value of "glory" from dying in the mouth of Homais? It is only by watching Flaubert reveal as barren the victory of radical philistines forced by their author to show their language as the "artificial mythologies" of a provincial world that Conrad can help James heroically drape "the robe of spiritual honor" around the "barren victories" of continually qualifying narrators of a saving romance.[38] The energetic morality of much ado by which Conrad and James held off the postmodernist political application of Flaubert's suspicion, directed against the need for moral romance, was made from the negotiations of distance with dupism.

Forced to "live in alien skins he hates" to earn the right to return after death as either a "panther" or a "star," Flaubert tries to disinfect himself from the need for romance; willingly present in the passion of familiar skins, Balzac returns to society for marriage to a rich noblewoman.[39] Shamelessly amateur in his free confusion of life and art, he is said to have called for the grace of his Dr. Bianchon on his deathbed; chastely professionally in their separation, Flaubert identifies with his Dr. Larivière, who enters the novel not only to scorn provincial distraction and stupidity, but to keep Madame Bovary's death punitively visible. James, characteristically, makes of *his* doctor, Sir Luke Strett, a tender watcher in the novel whose rather helpless presence is both judgment and a grace that keeps Milly's dying virtually invisible. What troubled Flaubert most was that Balzac's morality of identification, by which he paradoxically gave such liberty and genius to his characters, allowed them to embody his highest reveries, to expose them in story to all the guilts and attritions history had already prepared. His higher morality, in which he could enjoy the irresponsible beauty of his reveries out of the range of the cheap provincial "Beyond" of Madame Bovary, was to be immune to self-interest and base temptations stimulated by history. He can have nothing but disgust for Louise Colet when she poisons her poems with resentment against Alfred de Musset. And because he includes all personal opinion in his condemnation, it does not stretch us to imagine a rebuke to Balzac when he says it again: "I refuse to consider

38. Conrad, "A Familiar Preface," in *A Personal Record: Some Reminiscences*, 186. The phrase *artificial mythologies* is invented by Roland Barthes in *Mythologies*, 135, to describe Flaubert's conscious strategy to expose unconscious bourgeois mythology. JC, *Fic*, 87.

39. GF to Louise Colet, April 6, 1853, and Maxime du Camp, April 7, 1846, *Sel*, 151, 41. The image of doctor/artist as a tender watcher, whose generosity is manifested as freedom, is very close to the senior Henry James's description of God's relations to moral man. See William James's introduction to *The Literary Remains of the Late Henry James*, 35.

Art a drain-pipe for passion, a kind of chamberpot, a slightly more elegant substitute for gossip and confidence."[40]

The cold resistance of facts to all these passions and alibis is carried into the novels of James and Conrad as the justice of the real, but Flaubert makes clear, in his important correspondence with George Sand, that what he most dreaded was that his genius, if it was embodied as an artistic consciousness in the text and made vulnerable to all temptations of flesh, would suffer the same justice as the stupidity of Madame Bovary. Paradoxically, by this withdrawal, he forced modern novelists to treat *in* their fictions, *through* their artist figures, the question of how we live primarily as the question of how we can narrate, and how we judge as how we represent. Sand, missing in Flaubert's bourgeois novels an active and noble morality, provokes him to vehement response when she asks, "Why don't you put the figure of the artist in your work," making the question equivalent to "Why don't you put anything of your heart into what you write?" Flaubert's answer to this responds, as well, to Balzac's habit praised by Taine of giving to his men of genius his genius: "nothing good can be done with the character of the 'ideal Artist.' Art isn't intended to depict exceptional beings."[41] But he conveniently elides the infinite modes and gradations of Balzac's representations of talent tempted, seduced, and manipulated, naive inventors, angelic geniuses in the garrets of Paris, poets and sculptors of weak will, grand criminals. Balzac, as both a priestly and demonic force and a secretary of society, circulates in his novels as in history; Flaubert, a god of impersonality, invulnerable to bourgeois prayer and projection, only stares the moral scene into the tranquillity of the picturesque: "I feel an unconquerable aversion to putting anything of my heart on paper. I even think that a novelist *hasn't the right to express his opinion on anything*. God hasn't." Mademoiselle Vatnaz's description of the Bohemian entertainer Delmar suffers the humiliation of reduction to bourgeois and Romantic formulas naively joined and supported by Balzac: "He had a 'humanitarian soul; he understood the priestly role of the artist.'"[42]

The torment of style that Flaubert ceaselessly suffered as his martyrdom will nowhere be present in the work's classical surface, the glass ceiling for all bourgeois ambitions and aspirations arrested and, finally, merged. But the manifestation of authorial energy, melodramatically present in Balzac's opinions, becomes, in the novels of Conrad and James, the romantic morality of continuous effort, carrying its own criticism. The welter of composers and tellers in the novels, by their choices and discriminations,

40. GF to Louise Colet, January 9–10 and April 22, 1854, *Sel* 169, 175.
41. George Sand to GF, December 7 and November 30, 1866, and GF to George Sand, December 5–6 and 15–16, 1866, *Ltrs,* 92–95.
42. GF, *Sent,* 256; GF to George Sand, December 5–6, 1866, *Ltrs,* 93.

helps their creators to educate their best reveries to an active morality, forcing imagination and morality to a mutual responsibility and compromise. In this arrangement, the reader is lured out of the longing for Flaubert's mandarin peace, his condescension to bourgeois history, for the timeless permanence of the work become Nature. By immobilizing the educative possibilities of the bourgeoisie, whose good citizens, notes James, should not have kept him from dreaming in their midst, Flaubert wants to immobilize, as well, the reader on holiday from the constant work of moral sympathy: "What seems to me the highest in Art (and most difficult) is not to make you laugh or cry, nor to put you in rut or rage, but to act in the manner of nature, that is to *make you dream.* . . . Beautiful works . . . unmoving like cliffs, stormy like the ocean, full of foliage, greenery and murmurs like woods, sad like the desert, blue like the sky. Homer, Rabelais, Michelangelo, Shakespeare, and Goethe seem to me *pitiless.*"[43]

The paradoxes are only apparent: the novelist who accused Balzac's narrative of innocence was the secret seeker of purity; the best critic of the vices of the post-Romantic yearning for peace and permanence labored to achieve the transparency of the classical gaze as compensation for the collapse of principle into formula. If passion makes us historically impatient, the heart "like a branch, heavy with rain, trembl[ing] at the slightest tremor of the earth," art can force us to the "long patience" that helps us to rise above our "nervous susceptibilities," our religions, countries, social convictions. Whereas James's Balzac calms his susceptibilities by saturation, Flaubert's perpetrates the "exaltation of grace to the detriment of justice."[44] But why, asks James, does justice, both political and aesthetic, make Flaubert so furious at the "inevitable" and the "ephemeral?" Balzac's grace, his democracy of composer and character, kept justice from merely punishing those who deserved it without being worth it. Embarrassed by Balzac's adulteration of chemical with alchemical, dreaming of a great world of mythical pageantry and passion, forced to live in one entirely spoken by "artificial mythology" (HJ, "deFl," *Crit,* 2:313), Flaubert anticipated the protective pretense of the naturalist to adopt the pitiless professionality of contemporary science, climaxing in the intense visibility of pathology, surgery, and suicide.

43. The phrase *continuity of effort* is from Conrad, "Anatole France," *Fic,* 63; HJ, "deFl," *Crit,* 2:311. The phrase *moral holiday* is a favorite of William James; see WJ, *Plur,* 57, and *Truth,* 290. GF to Louise Colet, August 26, 1853; I use here the translation of Charles Bernheimer, *Flaubert and Kafka: Studies in Psychopoetic Structure,* 87.

44. GF to Louise Colet, August 21–22, 1853, and Mademoiselle Leroyer de Chantepie, March 18, 1857, *Sel,* 161–62, 195. The Franco-Prussian War aroused Flaubert's political ire against the times to such an extent that the antitheses justice and grace worked equally for historical as for aesthetic concerns. See GF to George Sand, April 30, 1871, *Ltrs,* 175–76.

Even as a young man, James had identified himself with the great *reader* of life to literature, Sainte-Beuve, and, now, as an American without a "national stamp," he hoped he could fashion a critical morality out of "a vast intellectual fusion and synthesis of the various National tendencies of the world." When, paralleling his brother's attack on the professionalism of philosophies and theologies by the amateur promotion of temperament, James targets the literal, undialectical, and reductive separatism of the naturalists (as he might, now, that of ideological academic schools), appropriating their methodology as image, he finds it useful to contrast the manner of Taine with that of Sainte-Beuve (though hardly easy on Balzac):

> The truth for M. Taine lies stored up, as one may say, in great lumps and blocks, to be released and detached by a few lively hammer blows; while for Sainte-Beuve it was a diffused and imponderable essence, as vague as the carbon in the air which nourishes vegetation, and, like it, to be disengaged by patient chemistry. His only method was fairly to dissolve his attention in the sea of circumstance surrounding the object of his study, and we cannot but think his frank provisional empiricism more truly scientific than M. Taine's premature philosophy.[45]

The novel's deep and complex truth could be honored only by yielding to its subtle magnetism of elective affinities, a magnetism charged by Balzac's rich appetite, his morality of dimension carried by a diction that infiltrates James's narratives and essays as "immense," "prodigious," "deep." Most revealing for his own practice, since Flaubert continually marshaled the blessing of facts against the curse of illusions, is James's emphasis on a patient disclosure of the contexts of the knowledge that traps both innocence and betrayal, giving romance the means to survive the curse of facts.[46] Sainte-Beuve stands in for those novelists like Conrad who rescue the morality of narrative by a deferential and "prolonged hovering flight of the subjective over the outstretched ground of the case exposed" from abbreviation by the most pointed and most told of methods: "The truly devout patience with which he kept his final conclusion in abeyance until after an exhaustive survey of the facts, after perpetual returns and ever-deferred farewells to them, is his living testimony to the importance of the facts." Against the Flaubertian standoff between private projection and public history, Conrad and James activate a continual and mutual stalking of fact and story, of the real and romance, of outer scene and psychic metaphor that prevents the novelist and the novelist as critic from "an inordinate

---

45. HJ to Thomas Sergeant Perry, September 20, 1867, *Ltrs,* 20; HJ, "Tain," *Crit,* 2:844.

46. Conrad's phrasing in his preface to *Almayer's Folly* (1895) is "The curse of facts and the blessing of illusions" (JC, *Fic,* 160).

haste to conclude" temperament's temptations and triumphs, from immunity to the truth that "resides in fine shades and degrees."[47] The courting of ambivalence in an atmosphere promoted by the American pragmatists, of the literal ever shadowed by the rhetorical, the Balzacian house by the house of fiction, conscience by consciousness, accounts for James's attraction to the phrase that is as much an American richness as poverty: *imagination of* loving, disaster, terror, morality.

To the extent that Zola flirts with the theory that science "applies us," his professional note taking is a danger. But as a great novelist, he demonstrated that "blue-books, reports, interviews" can only serve instinct: "vision and opportunity reside in a personal sense and a personal history, and no short cut to them in the interest of plausible fiction has ever been discovered." Balzac is more the master of the "waste of time, passion, of curiosity, of contact" that gives such authority to the world otherwise abbreviated by the economy of notes. When James laments the cost of Taine's "development in a single direction," he is warning of the loss to both criticism and fiction of a joyous dialectical competition between the satire of exposure and the morality of love, paradoxically promoted by the continuity in Balzac between ethics and the magic that metes out poetic justice and explains the universe. The conviction that obsessed the Sunday cenacle, that "held them together," was the need to stress that "art and morality are two perfectly different things and that the former has no more to do with the latter than it has with astronomy or embryology." James calls the hyperprofessionalism of "development in a single direction" an ignorance of "the precious art of compromise," but he implied, at a deeper level, that it was a cowardice at least equal to that of Anglo-American prudishness. The separation of art and morality, often assumed to be *his* credo, meant that morality could never be anything in the novel but conventional, all transgressions stereotyped or bestialized. James reminds Taine that, since English practitioners are "by disposition better psychologists," with a deeper imagination of morality, a morality that is free to play itself out in the amateur competitions of storytelling in the novel, they keep the "what of anything" from ever exhausting its resources in the "who."[48] That is why nothing in James seems beyond the range, finally, of that morality's educated guess.

47. HJ, "New," *Crit,* 1:149; "Tain," *Crit,* 2:844–45. Jean-Paul Sartre praises Conrad's moral use of the "resistance of words" in "François Mauriac and Freedom," *Literary Essays,* 21; henceforth cited as JPS, "Maur."

48. HJ, "Emile Zola" (1903), *Crit,* 2:891, 878; "Balz," *Crit,* 2:130; "deFl," *Crit,* 2:307; "Ivan Turgenev," *Crit,* 2:1014; "Zola's *Nana*" (henceforth cited as "Nana"), *Crit,* 2:870. Edel, *James,* 2:219. HJ, *The Notebooks of Henry James* (henceforth cited as *Note*), 18: "The *whole* of anything is never told."

Since his subject and reader, unlike those of Flaubert, are always free to "glory in a gap" between tellings, Conrad's undertaking is courageous in the manner of Balzac's surrender to the liberty of his characters. It ceaselessly works to keep internal resistance alive to his effort of fusing "what we are to know and that prodigy of our knowing." Sartre hailed this as modern morality by honoring the "resistance of words" of value (as against, we might claim, the fixity of the "mot juste" in fiction). Balzac helped the new novelist to shift morality to the active connections of composition between author and characters. Lucien's viewing of Coralie is his novelist's, ours, and that of the novel's entire cast of Parisian characters. The Anglo-American practitioner now must rescue metaphor from its Flaubertian isolation in the separate but equal stupidity of private projection or public rhetoric so that it can compensate for lost principle by serving as an agency of moral testing and communal binding. Again, it is Flaubert's great analyst Sartre who best describes the liberating compromise through the liberating of a word James educates as well in his novels: "Conrad suggests to us that Lord Jim may be 'romantic.' He takes great care not to state this himself; he puts the word into the mouth of one of his characters, a fallible being, who utters it hesitantly. The word 'romantic,' clear as it is, thereby acquires depth and pathos and a certain indefinable mystery." As an unprotected term consigned to the authority only of "amplitude and atmosphere," it conducts, by its adventures, both justice and grace. The hero of Sartre's *Nausea* confesses that it is our fate to be "always a teller of tales . . . surrounded by [our] stories and the stories of others."[49] But James and Conrad turn the vengeance of a "virtuoso" against exhausted language and ideas, thoroughly told by Flaubert, into an active morality of mutual listening, persuasion, and competition among author, character, and reader, and between character and character. Conrad takes us back to the Balzac of old sailing vessels for a moral metaphor of composition: "The modern ship is not the sport of the waves. Let us say that each of her voyages is a triumphant progress; and yet it is a question whether it is not a more subtle and more human triumph to be the sport of the waves and yet survive, achieving your end." That is why James returns his compliment: "You knock about in the wide waters of expression like the raciest and boldest of privateers." And Conrad might envy his Singleton's simple and profound morality of steering, mute, preliterary remnant of an old allegorical world, but he must stand, too, with the volatile, decadent, and sentimental consciousness of aspiring crews whose hovering between the "tender and complex," versions of "pity and distrust," "rage and humility," "doubt and certitude," "the desire of virtue and the fear of ridicule," "conceit and despair" seems

49. HJ, "New," *Crit,* 1:148–49; JPS, "Maur," 21; Jean-Paul Sartre, *Nausea,* 39.

to block momentum but finally propels it.[50] From Flaubert, Conrad learned the chilling corrective power of the spectacular and indifferent gaze of the universe, but he puts himself in the company of those struggling with a "vague and imperfect morality" to steer their stories, rich with rationalization and special pleading, to a provisional harbor.

The ironic context in which terms of moral value are rescued by the aesthetic of moral mystery clearly shows its initial debt to Flaubert: "And suddenly all the simple words they knew seemed to be lost forever in the immensity of their vague and burning desire. They knew what they wanted, but they could not find anything worth saying." Because the pathos of Madame Bovary's longing might exceed her story but not her stupidity, no accent can express her victory: "she makes of the business an inordinate failure, a failure which in turn makes for Flaubert the most *pointed,* the most *told* of anecdotes." The perilous ambivalence of ideal watchwords and psychological motive, compelled to continuous telling, keeps morality from being abbreviated to conventionality, physiology, and philistinism. James's evaluation of Feuillet is directed, as well, to the Parisian professionals under the sentence and complaint of exhausted material and language, unable to talk stories back to the novelist: "Men and women, in our conception, are deeper, more substantial, more self-directing; they have, if not more virtue, at least more conscience; and when conscience comes into the game human history ceases to be a perfectly simple tale."[51]

The energetic competition of storytellers as a moral measure is delightfully enacted by James's parodic version of Maupassant's famous and "perfectly simple tale": "The Necklace." "Paste" inverts the givens of the situation: the jewelry of a dead actress is deemed by her nephew worthless and turns out to be invaluable. The *fact* of worth, however, has the feel of an anticlimax to all the wonder, mystery, conjecture stirred by the sparkling storied facets of the jewelry. In his preface to "The Altar of the Dead" and other stories, James asks the question that is at the center of his morality, both in and out of the novel: about what does an author wonder? By linking this imagination to the moral sense in almost every preface and essay, he wars against the French refusal to liberate character to the morality that wonders about the author. Since all depends on "from whom it is hidden," the *"whole* of anything is never told," and this keeps the what from exhausting the who. It is striking to hear how often James links the word *mystery* to *morality.* Such a binding is the source of exuberant play, but it

50. GF to Louise Colet, September 4, 1852, *Sel,* 142; Conrad, *The Mirror of the Sea,* 70; HJ to Conrad, November 1, 1906, *Ltrs,* 368. Conrad, *The Nigger of the "Narcissus,"* 22, 23–25, 85; henceforth, cited as JC, *Nig.*

51. JC, *Nig,* 45, 82; Edel, *James,* 2:214–21, 3:95–106. HJ, "Bov," *Crit,* 2:323; "Nana," *Crit,* 2:870; "Feu," *Crit,* 2:285.

also serves as James's version of Conrad's tragic world "so painful with all sorts of wonder." Walking around the subject of *The Wings of the Dove,* for example, he lets the subject's spontaneous resistance to his presumptions mystify his attention and keep at bay his protection. He pretends to the "quality of bewilderment" that is the mark of his deepest characters, in the face of "the interesting possibilities and the attaching wonderments, not to say the insoluble mysteries," that "thicken apace." On behalf of his reader and character, James rescues Isabel Archer from Flaubert and the naturalists, though she may not, finally, thank him for it: "She would be an easy victim of scientific criticism if she were not intended to awaken on the reader's part an impulse more tender and more purely expectant."[52]

James proudly and humorously imagines, in his preface to *Daisy Miller,* a woman reader scolding him for letting his subject take such liberties with him: he is guilty of an "incurable prejudice in favour of grace." Conrad is partial, as well, to the presence of grace in a world and tale tormented by the fragmented reminders of old consoling allegories, though in such a wide universe it is sometimes beyond the range of his amateur tellers, his Marlow, to grant it or guess it out. The "Narcissus" has to sail through pages of ironic exposure of ideal terms and claims in order to receive it: "The sunshine of heaven fell like a gift of grace on the mud of the earth, on the remembering and mute stones, on greed, selfishness, on the anxious faces of forgetful men." It prepares for the necessary "sentimental lie" of the great ending, in which glamour, in all its begging, hyperbolic naïveté of expression, prevails.[53]

The most impoverishing reduction inflicted by the refusal of the French professionals to compromise is the obliteration of dramatic tensions, in the name of justice, between morality and the picturesque, terms that had tumbled through a long history of attraction and suspicion. Already working its way through contrasts with the sublime and beautiful, the picturesque was vulnerable to potential adulteration with the moral, in the touchy connections between the improvement of the estate and that of the soul, between the painting and the painter, between social color and social responsibility, the spectacular of Nature and the speculative of man. James and Conrad actively exploited the history of mutual tempting between the moral and the picturesque, forcing their flickering scenes of impressionist shades to serve as purgatories of ambivalence, tempting all tellers to alibi, because the Goncourts contended that Flaubertian "grammarians of the

52. HJ, "Preface to 'The Author of Beltraffio' et al.," *Crit,* 2:1242; "Preface to 'The Altar of the Dead,' et al.," *Crit,* 2:1257; "Maup," *Crit,* 2:530; *Note,* 18. JC, *Fic,* 82. HJ, "Wings," *Crit,* 2:1287; "Preface to *The Princess Casamassima*" (henceforth cited as "Casa"), *Crit,* 2:1092; "Wings," *Crit,* 2:1288; *Portrait of a Lady* (henceforth cited as *Portrait*), 105.
53. HJ, "Preface to *Daisy Miller,* et al.," *Crit,* 2:1271; JC, *Nig,* 106–7, 88.

Byzantine Empire" made of "idea" nothing but a "peg on which to hang sonorities of language" and light. In scenes of shadowy Maeterlinck coloring, James assumed Ruskin's designation of the picturesque as parasitical on a central place of value.[54]

The untested picturesque is actually compared by James, in a startling and clever counterthrust, to the sin of moralizing. Balzac's aesthetics of the grotesque are more instructive than his preaching because he saved the almost too vivid life of his picturesque by his saturation in temptation; George Sand, on the other hand, lacking moral taste as well, gives us the picturesque *of* morality, smoothing and harmonizing her texture into a sentimental climate of virtue. Yet, because she is not a "specialist," she avoids the Flaubertian fault of giving off, while withholding consciousness from character, "an indefinable impression of perverted ingenuity and wasted power" where the "sense of the picturesque has somehow killed the spiritual sense." In the naturalists, once representation is limited to the physiological, the moral problem is "contracted in order to meet it." The moral passivity of Flaubert's medium (the author's anger kept from the drama of temptation and education by the characters' stupidity) may be chosen, that of Maupassant's reflected, but it comes to the same refusal of compromise. The renunciation of the textual resistance provoked by Balzac's long rope of liberty leaves Flaubert's followers "morally stranded" and confined to "cold-blooded picturesques" whose "grotesque" faces and facts cannot be salvaged by Balzac's devotion to them. The goal of these specialists is to be "rare and precise about the dreadful."[55]

In a celebrated and powerful condolence letter that parallels William James's warning against the merging of the real and the ideal, Henry James praises the heroic resistance of consciousness to the temptations of mystic retreats from private and public pain. It is a letter we cannot imagine profiting Madame Bovary, but certainly his Isabel Archer:

> Don't melt too much into the universe, but be as solid and dense and fixed as you can. We all live together, and those of us who love and know, live so most. We help each other even unconsciously, each in our own effort, we lighten the effort of others, we contribute to the sum of success, make it possible for others to live. Sorrow comes in great waves—no one can know that better than you— but it rolls over us, and though it may almost smother us it leaves us on the spot, and we know that if it is strong we are stronger, inasmuch as it passes and we

---

54. *The Goncourt Journals: 1851–1870,* 45. Ruskin's attribution of mystery to genuine realism in his discussion of Turner in *Modern Painters* would also have attracted James. See chap. 2, n. 37.

55. Ruskin, "The Lamp of Meaning," in *Seven Lamps.* HJ, "Théâtre de Théophile Gautier" (henceforth cited as "Gau"), *Crit,* 2:357; "Sand," *Crit,* 2:698, 710–11, 730; "Bern," *Crit,* 2:181; "Maup," *Crit,* 2:543; "Tent," *Crit,* 2:294; "Bov," *Crit,* 2:340.

remain. It wears us, uses us, but we wear it and use it in return; and it is blind, whereas we after a manner see.[56]

The picture of Madame Bovary virtually falling into the opera might well be the lower version of the melting into the universe practiced by her author to escape the stupidity of modern morality. His preference for the beauty of ancient tyranny to the stupidity of modern fanaticism helps us to see how much he needed the strategy of merging all projections in the novel, what Jean Pierre Richard calls "the law of oozing," since he can even use it to connect his historical and provincial halves: "I'd like to show a civilized man who turns barbarian, and a barbarian who becomes a civilized man—to develop that contrast between two worlds that end up merging."[57]

The bristling discriminations cannot be collapsed in James's drama of morality and picture charged with the constant temptation to ritualize relationships, freezing the natural alternation between the vision of symbol (Bronzino portrait, dove) that "descends," as Woolf puts it, on people who recover their particularity. They were marshaled as well against the hazards of moral picturesque on the American side. If Howells, like the immature Isabel, papers over a perception of evil in reading private and national—American and Italian—histories, Hawthorne, a master painter of sin, resorts to a fancy palette for props and properties, and shadows, in his cultural and narrative innocence, his "inquisitive" side by the "evasive."[58] Though James might have taken mischievous delight in relaying to Howells the newly proposed Goncourt subject, a provincial whorehouse, he was glad to take his place with the American critics who, even while accusing him too of the wit and pessimism of the Paris cenacle, called on American writers to use the strengths of psychological and spiritual sensitivity for a morality that could make native Puritanism only a "heroic girdle."[59] As against the squeamishness of the "besotted mandarins" of French professionalism, our Anglo-American sensibilities, claims James, reflecting the spiritual and moral aestheticism of Arnold and Pater, "do not really react upon natural impressions and assert our independence until these impressions have been absorbed into our moral life and become a mysterious part of moral passion." That dimension, missing in Daudet, the master of picturesque, because he had no "natural understanding of the religious passion," is a holy place for the son of Henry James, Sr., for whom

56. HJ to Grace Norton, July 28, 1883, *Ltrs,* 191.
57. Jean-Pierre Richard, "The Creation of Form in Flaubert," 47.
58. Woolf, *To the Lighthouse,* 72. HJ, "William Dean Howells," *Crit,* 1:504; "Review of *Italian Journeys,*" *Crit,* 1:476; "Hawthorne," *Crit,* 1:363, 360.
59. Edel, *James,* 2:16; Thomas Wentworth Higginson, from *Atlantic Monthly,* 1870, in Richard Ruland, ed., *A Storied Land: Theories of American Literature,* 2:20.

morality's narrowing tendency to arrogance was always to be humbled by the widening spirit. The spiritual dimension of morality scorned, so too are the rich compromises negotiated between the visible and the invisible world: "Even a style rich in similes is limited when it renders only the visible. The invisible Flaubert scarcely touches. . . . He had no faith in the power of the moral to offer a surface."[60]

The deliberate appropriation of the plane of the picturesque for moral depth is a sign of how much James depended upon the interaction of the two levels to give a socializing and discriminating power to metaphor denied to the desolately impotent and supplementary simile of Flaubert. A central image of compromised composition climaxes the preface to *The Wings of the Dove*. The enjoyment of a work of art is "greatest, it is delightfully, divinely great when we feel the surface, like the thick ice of the skater's pond, bear without cracking the strongest pressure we throw on it." The counterleveling of democratic juxtaposition, the critical design of Flaubert's syntax, collapses the tension between these planes. When his student Maupassant practices his teacher's exercise of staring at a tree so patiently he closes off the invisible, he lands in an aesthetic professionalism that "skips the whole reflective part which governs conduct and produces character." If these pessimists of passive fate have captured the attention of the hour, the optimists of moral discrimination, "the writers for whom the life of the soul is equally real and visible (lends itself to effects and triumphs, challenges the power to 'render')," are "formidable competitors" waiting in the wings (HJ, "Wings," *Crit*, 2:1301; "Maup," *Crit*, 2:547–48, 504). They have the mission to make the quality and intensity of seeing the premise of personal and communal morality.

To call attention to the distinction between those who render on one or two planes, James calls his own morality "mysterious" and that of the naturalists merely "mystifying," a term that purposively affronts the naturalist pride in clarity. To the contention that all motive should be unavailable to description, James, always working for his characters of high consciousness as fellow composers, replies: "From whom is it hidden? From some people, no doubt, but very much less from others." As a novelist, "it is

60. Edel, *James*, 4:105. HJ, "Gau," *Crit*, 2:378; "Alphonse Daudet" (1883), *Crit*, 2:248; "deFl," *Crit*, 2:312. James's complaint against the Flaubertian school parallels this of Matthew Arnold in his 1873 preface to *Literature and Dogma*: the German Bible critics have helped English readers by their negative criticism but have left them stranded by countering with no positive power to preserve the healthy spiritual morality of the Bible that needs to be absorbed by a rich and responsive English imagination (see *Complete Prose Works*, 6:157–58). But James's bristling consubstantiality of the real and romantic is not as ambitious and optimistic a cultural agent as Arnold's synthesis of imaginative reasonableness. The crossroads of conscience and consciousness is, in James, a meeting of one on one.

as difficult to describe an action without glancing at its motive, its moral history, as it is to describe a motive without glancing at its practical consequence."[61] Where Flaubert and his disciples see the dangerous potentiality of seduction into sentimentality and philistine moralism, James sees a renunciation of the full energy, subtlety, and drama of rendering. To make things more difficult for justice while honoring its authority as purveyor of merciless fact, James and Conrad let giddy projections of self- idealization, innocent and intimate as "the happy language of exaggeration" before the deed, wander into murky labyrinths of alibi, ambivalence, and suppressions, opening, at last, to the "charged stillness" where they have everything to lose and to gain. Henrietta Stackpole's anxiety that Isabel Archer's new fortune might expose her on the moral side is intimately related both to Isabel's anxiety and interest in an expanded imagination of herself, in her own eyes and in the eyes of others, and to James's concern, noted in his preface, to made her "*disponible.*" The famous "house of fiction" is not a place of fairy tales; it is Milly's "whole bright house of [cosmopolitan] exposure," through which we walk to bring our romances to the right place, the place of depth, where no Osmond can reach us. The favorite James metaphor for the medium at its climax, in both novels and criticism, is that of a spreading tide. Because Balzac had immersed himself "up to his chin . . . in his illusion," Conrad's medium is the "residuum" of a "wandering, circling, yearning imaginative *faculty,* encountered in its habit as it lives and diffusing itself as a presence or a tide." In like manner, when Densher finds himself sinking in Milly's medium, the rising tide of her grace that moves him to justice, the "dove" as simile is liberated from its ungenerous manipulation by an immature and irresponsible politics of language, which had charged the novel with noise, into a metaphor of moral imagination, assuring us that no protagonist will waste James's faith. But the driving and cruel wit of Kate's original plan to have everything, an unconditioned life, does, finally, by its brutality to Milly's story, become "a tragic waste of effort," like that of the professional Flaubert in relation to the story of Madame Bovary.[62]

Though James and Conrad honored Flaubert's "rage" of effort to hide it in a classical texture, they were intent upon making that sustained effort everywhere apparent in their narrations as an active moral agent of testing and qualification. While Flaubert strands occasional questions like "What was the meaning of it" in a mind and air drained of wonder and desire for interpretation, they are busy rescuing morality from all that

61. HJ, "Maup," *Crit,* 2:529–30. Elsewhere I have discussed Ibsen's legacy to James of a morality of depth and mystery; see Naomi Lebowitz, *Ibsen and the Great World.*

62. HJ, *Dove,* 97, 469; *Portrait,* 267, 275; "Wings," *Crit,* 2:1301; "Lady," *Crit,* 2:1075; *Portrait,* 100; "Balz," *Crit,* 2:128; "New," *Crit,* 1:151; "Bov," *Crit,* 2:327.

would "cheat it of its legitimate terrors" and temptations, cut short, as if guillotined, from its wide relations and combinations. In this way, medium and metaphor carry a moral imagination wide enough to harbor, with justice and grace, all the "half-truths, half-thoughts, whole illusions of existence," wringing finally "a meaning from our sinful lives." It needs to be a sustained effort to provisionally allay "the doubt of the sovereign power enthroned in a fixed standard of conduct" that disappointed Flaubert into martyrdom.[63] For James, the compromise carried by the medium of the moral imagination is the marriage of the real and the romantic (what his Milly presciently calls "the larger 'real'"), in Flaubert, so unfruitfully and punitively set against each other or living side by side as mere dualities. The marriage is blessed by the "responding imagination" of Balzac (sometimes dangerously romantic to his admirer Howells, defender of a *healthy* realism), immersing himself and us in a current "extraordinarily rich and mixed" and washing "us successively with the warm wave of the near and familiar and the tonic shock . . . of the far and strange." Either dimension may carry the contest of the "real" and "romantic" since, like all evaluative terms, like all stories, they are forced to guess at each other, tempt each other, betray and enrich each other *in* and *between* characters. Here is the celebrated definition James worked into all his novels:

> The real represents to my perception the things we cannot possibly *not* know, sooner or later, in one way or another; it being but one of the accidents of our hampered state, and one of the incidents of their quantity and number, that particular instances have not yet come our way. The romantic stands, on the other hand, for the things that, with all the wealth and all the courage and all the wit and all the adventure, we never *can* directly know; the things that can reach us only through the beautiful circuit and subterfuge of our thought and our desire.[64]

The compromised way of knowing, by which James both curses and blesses his finest "centres of consciousness," is of the spiritual kind that starts with love and bewilderment and widens into the mysterious and deep imagination of morality. The hypostatizing and sensationalizing of the relation between the real and the romantic in Flaubert is what keeps justice from educating bullying ideal projections out of what D. H. Lawrence calls their possessive materialism,[65] which fetishizes people into ma-

---

63. HJ, "Bov," *Crit*, 2:316; Conrad, *Lord Jim*, 40, 31; JC, *Nig*, 107; JC, "Alphonse Daudet," *Fic*, 55. The posture that both suffers and survives an irony trying to defeat the final cry of *The Nigger of the "Narcissus"* and *Lord Jim*'s "one of us" (a sign of a positive fellowship of illusion rather than a negative one of stupidity) would be attractive to Richard Rorty's "liberal ironist," the hero of his *Contingency, Irony, and Solidarity*.

64. HJ, *Dove*, 160; "Bov," *Crit*, 2:321; "Preface to *The American*," *Crit*, 2:1062–63.

65. *Psychoanalysis and the Unconscious*, 12.

chines. It leads into a brutal naturalism, a kind of knowing obviously perpetrated by the fact-bound Lord Mark, but, more surprisingly, by the imaginative Kate who sells out her bewilderment to plot. Naturalistically abused, she naturalistically "handles."

That James continually, like Conrad, brought into the novels a respect and rebuke of the naturalists of both style and subject can clearly be seen in the overconditioned opening scene of *The Wings of the Dove,* a scene that tempts Kate, Densher, and the reader, all through the novel, to moral alibi. The move to Mrs. Lowder's medium gives stimulus to the self-idealizing drive toward a "saving romance" by offering a totally new set of circumstances, a new "language of the house," that allows Kate even to humor her beginnings. It makes possible a "happy language of exaggeration" she secretly shares with Densher, a Balzacian riot of biological and economic epithet (no longer licensed as narrative innocence), swelling the form of Mrs. Lowder. But it starts, as well, the languages of the American princess, Mrs. Lowder, and Susan Stringham, like Kate, hungry for "everything." Since James makes Kate such an attractive and energetic composer, we are constantly affronted by the picture of her in her father's house; she makes us want her to try for everything, to feel, as with our Balzac hero, how much each aesthetic and political choice matters, and we are, like Densher, in awe of the will behind her willingness to do what she doesn't like for the sake of that everything: "It wasn't till afterwards that, going back to it, he was to read into this speech a kind of heroic ring, a note of character that belittled his own incapacity for action." Continually James tests his terms in the rhetorical contests they are forced to conduct. The fairy-tale heroism of waiting and working for the sake of having, at last, everything is not, it turns out, the heroism that will float morality into the larger tide of spiritual imagination. The great educative irony turns, in this passage, on the misunderstanding of the nature and order of spiritual knowing as a mode of making authentic morality out of aesthetic opportunity.

We know we owe the novel's dramatic richness to the imaginative energy of Kate's desire, not to Densher's willingness to settle for "being as we are." The irony of justice becomes more brutal in relation to the story of another, Milly: "'She's scared. She has so much to lose. And she wants more.' 'Ah well,' said Densher with a sudden strange sense of discomfort, 'couldn't one say to her that she can't have everything?' 'No—for one wouldn't want to'" (HJ, *Dove,* 102, 105, 97, 395, 282, 102). James, in the manner of Kierkegaard, leads Milly to the spiritual climax that both follows and reverses the fairy-tale measure by drawing gain out of loss. Her grace—which ultimately lets Densher off, but only to his agonized conscience, by granting to the spreading medium immunity to the complicitous language of plotting—yields us what no single character can have: everything. It has earned its authority by entertaining all the mutual linguistic lures, baits, and blocks of "felt life" between the romance and real of histories, American abysses and European labyrinths, of tiered society and a "thumping bank note," of national identities and houses, of sickness and health without closing off the amateur compromises that were such anathema to the professionalism of the "French literary mind of the day."[66] And its "mot juste" is the obsessively repeated and redundant diction of "deep depth" that signals a transferred language of impasse dear to D. H. Lawrence, on the threshold of great spiritual value. It is a diction that binds the visible to the invisible, the dead to the living in an expansive relation and education made only sentimental by a mourning Charles Bovary.

The French mind is honored in the checked power of authorial sympathy restricted to the pathos of a tender watcher surrounded by stories who, in the body of a Susan Stringham, fearful of not being able to leave romantic material untouched, must decrease so his princess may increase. Against Flaubert, and in the manner of Balzac, James allows Ralph Touchett to put his genius into play by challenging the "requirements" of Isabel's imagination with his own. But he characteristically left the compositional interest of even as tender a surrogate watcher as Ralph open, in his "imagination of loving," to the temptation of greedy curiosity—open enough, in fact, to attract a reproach of "immoral" from Ralph's father and Henrietta Stackpole. And the mind of Taine is honored, in *The Wings of the Dove,* especially in the scene in the National Gallery, with the legitimate, if rationalized, relief from "the personal question" by recourse to national type and image. But Naturalism's stimulation, in Kate's mind, of the "imagination of terror" is dwarfed by the final medium of the imagination of morality that frees us to the possibility and responsibility of enduring our conditioning with generosity. It is the imagination, suggests James in his preface to *The Portrait of a Lady,* that "converts" the glorious distraction of Europe, pictured in the first pages, from the outer drama of an international crossing to the international inner drama of both author and character. And leading Isabel, James, as much as Kafka, fashioned a thorough commensurability between cultural atmospheres and arguments he lived in and psychic ones he carried in him from his early family romance. The "deep difficulty" can be "braved" only by composers who, "finely aware and richly responsible,"[67] bind conscience to consciousness. The willingness to be a dupe of the

66. HJ, *Dove,* 71. The punishing force of Romance infiltrating a smaller consciousness was one of the strokes James admired in George Eliot's *Daniel Deronda*: HJ, "Conversation on Daniel Deronda," *Crit,* 1:990; "Loti," *Crit,* 2:510.

67. HJ, *Dove,* 126–27, 239, 167, 386; *Portrait,* 237; "Lady," *Crit,* 2:1079; "Casa," *Crit,* 2:1088. For Balzac as a tender and paternal protector of liberty, see HJ, "Balz," *Crit,* 2:132.

responsibility that life and art owe each other, with the certainty of compromised "everything," is the amateur heroism that, for Bakhtin, makes
fate a freedom. Taine characterized Balzac as a man in debt while James
saw him as a novelist who had paid his debt. Joyce, who puts this debt into
every chapter of the "great and trivial" *Ulysses* as both fact and metaphor,
plays the Balzac in Bloom, whose eyes liberate all he looks upon, against
the Flaubert in Stephen. Bloom's guilty, defensive, and curious subjectivity,
socially exiled, paradoxically opens up for us a place of public health, even
if we cannot yet move into it. But it is Stephen who reminds us to free the
wandering Jew from the pathology of an impotent sentimentality by quot-
ing Meredith against his naturalist mocker, Mulligan: "The sentimentalist
is he who would enjoy without incurring the immense debtorship for a
thing done."[68] The artist, split between them, ransoms both justice and
grace.

Flaubert is the great, demolishing dreamer of the modern novel, and he
renounced the joy of composition to incur his debt; but by refusing to lead
his characters into a battle worthy of him, James implies, he sentimen-
talized morality. He forced the bracketing of heroic effort and crude advice
and opinion in Balzac's novels but could not prevent James from assenting
to the imperative interpretation in Isabel's and Milly's great, still nights of
consciousness, to Milly's musing on Mrs. Lowder, loved by her author as
Balzac loved his Valérie: "Idealists, in the long run, *don't* feel that they
lose." Leaving in their wake, like Milly, herself, "however briefly and bro-
kenly, the sense of having lived," they reward the great effort of James and
Conrad to strike, through all recorded derision, "the accent of heroic truth,"
to render "the heroic effort to live *expressed* / As victory."[69]

---

68. HJ, "Balz," *Crit,* 2:130. The novelistic heroism is everywhere emphasized in M. M.
Bakhtin's *The Dialogic Imagination* and *Problems of Dostoevsky's Poetics.* In the first
page of *Lost Illusions,* Balzac calls his story a "grande petite histoire," simultaneously
great and trivial; James Joyce, *Ulysses,* 164.
69. It is interesting to compare this assumption with that of Nietzsche concerning
Flaubert—that loathing of man is linked to an impotent pity (*Beyond Good and Evil,*
147). James's grace is too hard for pity. D. H. Lawrence, "Georgian Poetry: 1911–1912," in
Phoenix, 304: "It was a dream of demolition." HJ, *Dove,* 157; "Wings," *Crit,* 2:1287; *Dove,*
196: "I shall never be better than this." Conrad, *Personal Record,* 186. "Reply to Papini,"
in WS, *Poems,* 446.

4

THE PURGATORY OF PLOT

Rousseau and Balzac

His judgement admitted no purgatory.

André Gide

Not the least of literature's blessings is that it offers artists an intriguing and legitimate labyrinth, the purgatory of plot, to reach public virtue by working through private resentments. It provides its practitioners with hundreds of disguises for the vengeful motive, winds a way from shameful personal anger to innocent and powerful claims made in the human interest. We recognize the conversion even when we have to take it on faith in Shakespeare and Tolstoy, who disappear into their works as if they had been born blessed with unquestioned rights to love and outrage. Virginia Woolf notes the freedom from personal vengeance in this type: "The reason perhaps why we know so little of Shakespeare . . . is that his grudges and spites and antipathies are hidden from us. We are not held up by some 'revelation' which reminds us of the writer. All desire to protest, to preach, to proclaim an injury, to pay off a score, to make the world the witness of some hardship or grievance was fired out of him and consumed. Therefore his poetry flows from him free and unimpeded."[1] Doubtless, it is this sense of perfect assimilation that lured Joyce's Stephen to his elaborate biographical grounding of the bard. In the best amateur tradition, Woolf tries to navigate her guilt over the possible evidence of personal motives of anger and spite in her literature, felt as a steady and subtle discomfort between the aesthetic and moral, by acknowledging continually her conditioning as

1. *A Room of One's Own*, 99.

an institutionally deprived daughter of educated fathers and brothers. The task makes her sensitive to traces, in George Eliot, of "the vindictiveness of a grudge which we feel to be personal in its origin," when she moves, in her literature, out of her class—but we assume, too, that, in Woolf, it has to do with moving out of her gender. The line of patriarchal writers has its privileges of professional power. But the question of negative capability is a tricky business. If we are tempted to assume that the fiction of the magically unconscious genius of Hardy seems less vulnerable to vindictive vestiges than the novels carrying the self-conscious genius of Henry James, which sometimes "tortures" and "wearies" the reader,[2] still, the patterns of exclusion that marked the life of the American novelist are generously displaced into growth of consciousness in the finest characters and readers, a democratic negotiation of outrage and resentment, as knowledge becomes its own punishing reward.

The modern strain of anxiety associated with the surfacing of personal motive in the novel might have its origins in the much analyzed duplicities of Rousseau's magnetic *Confessions,* where the philosopher's "folly," in the sharp judgment of the novelist François Mauriac, manifests itself as a dour and unsociable refusal to "establish any relationship between his love of virtue and the meanness of his life," while he wore "himself out in the desire to resolve such a contradiction."[3] The inventor of the Subjective Universal had, in contradistinction to Montaigne, to make his body as uniform, permanent, consistent, and innocent as Truth, Justice, Equality unadulterated by the wit and wickedness of city philosophers and salons. Not for him Montaigne's tolerance of the "consubstantiality" of "good and evil with our lives" (M, 3:13.835). The fear surfaces most strongly in an obsessive disclaimer of personal motives of vengeance against an exclusive society, a vengeance that threatens to mar Rousseau's alliance of personal innocence and public truth and to force him to honor, in the amateur mode, his offensive as much as his defensive instincts. An apostrophe in the *Letter to M. d'Alembert on the Theatre* clearly separates pure and holy truth from the needs of a vengeance continually kept alive by exclusions and compulsively sublimated into counterexclusions: "Holy and pure truth . . . my pen will refuse thee only what it fears to accord to vengeance."[4]

An even more powerful drive in Rousseau's work is the urge to make vengeance innocent by making innocence, innocence alone, his vengeance.

---

2. Woolf, "George Eliot," in *Common Reader,* 1:240; and see Woolf's comment on Charlotte Brontë's anger in *A Room of One's Own,* 78; "Thomas Hardy," in *Common Reader,* 2:269; "Mr. Henry James's Latest Novel," in *Essays,* 1:23.

3. "Jean-Jacques Rousseau," in *Men I Hold Great,* 312.

4. Jean-Jacques Rousseau, *Politics and the Arts: Letter to M. d'Alembert on the Theatre,* 132n; henceforth cited in the text as JJR, *Ltr.*

When, in the third Reverie, Rousseau credits his own innocence as the best resource by which to convert vengeful motives, he only reminds us of the countless mechanisms by which he attempts to free it from social compromise, not the least of which is confession because it rejects the disguises of those moral and aesthetic plots in life and literature, patently driven by vengeance. Rousseau's inquisitor in the second preface to *La Nouvelle Héloise* had directly reproached the novel for its flouting of fiction's normal interests; it has no bad actions, no bad situations, no bad men. And in his own person, in *The Confessions,* Rousseau answers this persona and Diderot, who praised Richardson's variety and number of scenes and characters, by claiming a superior virtue for the situation untainted by "marvellous adventures."[5] Rousseau well knew what Balzac would later assume as inevitable, that action in the social world of cities like Paris, in life and in books, was implicated in the stirring up and executing of vengeance, especially if the actor is an artist tormented by the politics of rank and power. Knowing we, as readers of plot, would have to wait too long and tediously in garrets to reap the virtuous vengeance of genius with a strong character, the domination of society by his vivid literature, Balzac, the fully vulnerable novelist, pretends to wish for a way to unite monochromatic integrity and the aesthetically magnetic and self-interested plotting of Madame Marneffe, pushed on by an excluded Cousin Bette: "Imagine a virtuous Madame Marneffe, . . . and you have the Marchesa de Pescara!"[6] Rousseau was too terrified a moralist to risk such musing. But Balzac, who loved to depict aesthetically the plots he ethically censured, giving equal value, if not time, to both sides, could assume that the vow of vengeance, his purloined letter, could be dramatically deployed as a legitimate motive of both good and bad ambitions. In this way, open on all sides, it could work itself free from its origins in a socially greedy genius. He knew, as well, that long and sensuous stories of seduced talents in a Paris of prostituted professions, picturesquely unique and morally identical, could serve as protest and stir a need, if not an interest, in the reader for a sight of the garret. By shamelessly putting the personality of his genius in his work, threading it through labyrinthine plots, he was able to distinguish the spectacular vengeance of the artist as dandy from the legitimate vengeance of great depicters of humanity and to justify it as power beyond resentment and spite.

But how could Rousseau, as suspicious of the negotiations between the dupe and the master as between aesthetic and ethical instincts, handle his moral and ontological fear of plotting both in and out of his writings? For, in his mind, the machinations of the persecuting Paris clique were linked

5. *The Confessions,* 505; henceforth cited in the text as JJR, *Conf.*
6. Balzac, *Cousin Bette,* 299; henceforth cited in the text as HB, *Cou.*

to those of seductive stories that trapped his worst traits, vitiated his style, and contaminated his morality. Plot too readily draws innocence to unassimilated vengeance in one both sexually timid and passionate. So much need for maternal love, so much fear of his own aggression and of the power of women in love, so much guilt for the birth that killed his mother and for his own filial sexuality, so much resentment of his social inferiority—these might never find a way out of the labyrinths of bad actions. He must not cooperate with plotters if he is to represent innocence. When Thérèse reveals that Madame d'Epinay is playing games with Rousseau's love for Madame d'Houdetot, the love that typically found its climax in *La Nouvelle Héloise,* Rousseau confesses: "My indignation and fury [were] beyond description. Instead of dissembling with Mme d'Epinay, after her own fashion, and resorting to counterplots [*contre-ruses*], I yielded unreservedly to the impetuosity of my nature and, with my usual heedlessness, burst out quite openly" (JJR, *Conf,* 418). Rousseau could not enjoy or admit the need of story to make its ethics out of candor by making its aesthetics out of secrets.

Without the sublimating passion for plot, Rousseau characteristically resorts to declamation—"persecuted innocence will find a defender" (JJR, *Conf,* 419)—or to the reassurance that his "frankness" will "overcome" the enemy's "subtlety," even to the point of convincing her of her wrong (JJR, *Conf,* 420). Nothing so frustrated Rousseau as the air of surprise and indifference on the faces of the guilty enemies, like the brutal and cunning Baron Grimm; but are his descriptions persuasive when they resent story? Since the whole of *The Confessions* is a diatribe against mystery, plot, and plotting, when its author recognizes himself in a position from which he could take cruel revenge—against Madame d'Epinay, for example, were she to discuss openly the matter of his children's placement in a foundling home (JJR, *Conf,* 437), an abandonment that must have gradually felt like an imitation of his own abandonment by a dead mother and an exiled father—he must transform these feelings into open testimonies of innocence. Would not even those children, heirs to inequality and exile, a cause of public outrage, have hated and betrayed their parents (JJR, *Conf,* 333)? He can displace guilt by mocking Montaigne's "false ingenuousness, . . . his pretence of confessing his faults while taking good care only to admit to likeable ones"; and there is some smugness in the comparison to his own case: "I, who believe, and always have believed, that I am on the whole the best of men, felt that there is no human heart, however pure, that does not conceal some odious vice" (JJR, *Conf,* 479). We suspect pride in revelation when we remember that innocence, in life as in literature, is not a problem for Montaigne, for whom original sins of human reason and feeling are counted as original maladies. No one who did not dream of vengeance often could have spoken so obsessively of having no interest in it; the odious motive, present in Rousseau from the beginning, is neutralized by plotlessness until it reaches the Nietzschean resolution of the sixth Reverie, which is not that impressive since we have only partial powers and partial stories: Rousseau would have been the kindest and best of men if he had been the most powerful, and in order to annihilate in himself all desire for vengeance, it would have sufficed to be *able* to avenge himself.[7]

This claim betrays a major design throughout Rousseau's writings. The guilt-ridden suppression of stirrings of vengeance, the pretense of not feeling hate, is converted into innocent, because necessary, counterexclusions. The son kills the mother in childbirth, so he comes to feel that the mother excludes him. This "bad situation"—Rousseau's favorite term for places of crossed interest, in which desire is socially stimulated to betray virtue—is reinforced by all the agonized splits in the social world between appearance and being, by false accusations over combs and ribbons, by bad apprenticeships, oppressive conversations, and conventions. In the social world, we must kill to be born into power. If talk in the Paris salon is witty competition, if it humiliates the awkward provincial, excludes or distorts him (always *after* entry), the guilt that hangs on subsequent motives of counterexclusion must be turned into the innocence of counterexclusion by necessity. It is soothed by apostrophe, confession, reverie, all forms of discourse that scorn competitive games of power, refusing return: "I do not know whether my heart could subdue its hatred, for it has never felt any; and I think too little about my enemies to claim the merit of forgiving them . . . they have absolute power, and they use it. There is only one thing beyond their reach . . . it is, by tormenting themselves about me to make me torment myself about them" (JJR, *Conf,* 540–41). It is no wonder that Kierkegaard and so many other readers sensitive to theological structures see the problem of egoism in a Rousseau without a Christian recourse to grace. Rousseau's writings are burdened with the special pleading that is gleefully exposed again and again by critics who are, nevertheless, seduced by the dream behind the apology, the dream of man free of original sin.

The most essential testing ground of literature is the bad situation, the situation that tempts its victim into brothels of betrayal and disappointment. Rousseau exposes these as places of inequality and exclusion, in government, theaters, salons, false friendships. While Balzac revels in the immersion, Rousseau must move joylessly through bad situations and ruin plots by defenses of innocence, primarily those that work us all back to a common regressive recovery of a *good* situation, of the sweet, unmediated

7. Rousseau, *The Reveries of the Solitary Walker,* 81–82; henceforth cited in the text as JJR, *Rev.*

confession, in the presence of mama (JJR, *Conf,* 197, 250). Is not the entire *Confessions,* compelled by the world's misunderstanding, persecution, exile, itself a bad situation avenged by the child it ruined? After leading us slowly and painfully through social hell, one that constantly stirs sensations of vengeance, acknowledged only enough to justify escape, Rousseau rushes us past purgatory to Nature, a place of maternal communion that corrects the guilty birth, where "there is no cunning and rascally man to thrust himself between" (JJR, *Conf,* 594). The notorious "exception to Nature's laws" (JJR, *Conf,* 595) is received, included, and embraced by the very mother the capitol had abandoned. She even allows Rousseau the playful fantasy of innocent power ("I dispose of all Nature as its master" [R, *Conf,* 158]), a luxury of guiltless inequality. In the struggle to make his situation into his element, Rousseau must clear it of vengeance. In sophisticated society, far from the sweet society of the country, he could rarely avoid situations that might set his interest in opposition to some other man's and cause him, despite himself, to wish that person ill (JJR, *Conf,* 62). If he, so sensitive to the frustrations of his interests, were to choose to go against them for the sake of a common interest, what better proof could he give of a devotion to truth so strong, so scornful of paltry vengeance, that it can return civilization to virtue? His diatribe against the dangers of theater, written in the country, away from men, reminds us that its author is both true and innocent because, personally, he loves plays and dislikes dance. What is virtue unassayed? Such a test and transformation is Rousseau's love for Madame d'Houdetot, of which he notes: "the very strength of the feelings which might have made us guilty was the reason for our remaining innocent" (JJR, *Conf,* 446). It is no wonder that Rousseau must rest in those places of retreat, the country, Les Charmettes, the provinces of song where feelings only personal in origin become divorced from personal interests without the ardent transformation necessary in the city, or in salons of country estates, in the name of Injustice, Inequality, Exclusion (JJR, *Conf,* 30). Not for Rousseau the pleasures of the perverted nephew of Rameau, whom his treacherous friend Diderot pins to the corrupt social world that, by conditioning his art, compensates "for loss of innocence by loss of prejudices."[8] The prejudices that cling to Rousseau's innocence, declared in the world, are transformed into universals, not stories, of justice.

The continuous and tiring transformation of bad situations into good ones to disguise vengeance against a world that practices exclusions must be achieved without the normal ruses of fiction. If Rousseau writes a novel, it must become a good situation, in which sexual exclusion (perhaps a problem of inequality, a father's pride, or a problem of psychological timid-

---

8. Diderot, *"Rameau's Nephew" and "d'Alembert's Dream,"* 81.

ity, perversion, fear) is reversed while the fulfillment remains innocent, superior to the society and psychology that frustrated it. The figures of fantasy, unlike the children of Thérèse who might have remained in the home, or Parisian friends, will neither counterbetray nor abandon their author, but, protected from secret plots, will lead him to virtue. The novel must contain this confession: "The first, the greatest, the strongest, the most inextinguishable of all my needs was entirely one of the heart. It was the need for intimate companionship, for a companionship as intimate as possible, which was the chief reason why I needed a woman rather than a man, a woman friend rather than a man friend. This singular need was such that the most intimate physical union could not fulfill it; only two souls in the same body would have sufficed. Failing that, I always felt a void" (JJR, *Conf,* 386). Beyond class, sexual passion is always unequal because of the great power of women in the empire of love (JJR, *Ltr,* 47), so Saint-Preux falls in love with the relationship between Claire and Julie: "No, nothing, nothing on earth is capable of exciting so voluptuous a tenderness as your mutual caresses, and in my eyes, the sight of two lovers might have offered a less delightful sensation."[9] The family romance is rendered guiltless by a willing participation in a ménage à trois. Thus, *because* Rousseau is forced to overcome his feelings of rivalry with Anet, he sees the pattern like this: "Our every wish and care and affection was held in common, none of them extending outside our own little circle. Our habit of living together, to the exclusion of the outer world, became so strong that if one of the three was missing from a meal or a fourth person joined us, everything was spoiled" (JJR, *Conf,* 194). In book 6 of *The Confessions,* Rousseau tells the story of how a concentration on disinterested virtue, with which he would also endow the usurper, Wintzenried, helped him to overcome feelings of rejection, abandonment, betrayal, and subsequent vengeance (JJR, *Conf,* 248). So inequality and exclusion, adultery and snobbery, the heart and soul of both social and aesthetic plots, are neutralized.

Rousseau's Platonic anxiety that he might allow himself to be seduced into his novel, potentially a bad situation, serves, out of his own body, the body politic. We have seen how he converts, for the sake of an idealized Nature, his mother and the proper mother of civilization, a natural sexual passion by an unnatural displacement through recourse to renunciation and the trinity: "My voluptuous imaginings would have lost all their grace if they had lacked the gentle colors of innocence" (JJR, *Conf,* 405). Wary of

9. Rousseau, *La Nouvelle Héloise: Julie, or the New Eloise,* 96; henceforth cited in the text as JJR, *Nouv.* See also Tony Tanner's discussion of *La Nouvelle Héloise* in *Adultery in the Novel: Contract and Transgression,* 113–78. For some semiotic implications of erotic spying, fantasizing, gazing in Rousseau, Balzac, Flaubert, and James, see Peter Brooks, *Body Work: Objects of Desire in Modern Narrative.*

the power cherished by novelists, Rousseau confesses to us the origin of the scene in which Saint-Preux purges his passion in the friendship of Julie and Claire: "I imagined two women friends, rather than two of my own sex, since although examples of such friendships are rarer they are also more beautiful. . . . I allowed of no rivalry or quarrels or jealousy because I find it hard to imagine any painful feelings, and I did not wish to discolour my charming picture with anything degrading to Nature. Being captivated by my two charming models, I identified myself as far as I could with the lover and friend" (JJR, *Conf,* 400–401). Because the love of Madame d'Houdetot and Saint-Lambert for each other threatens to exclude him, Rousseau feels more than usual the necessity that fiction renounce its power to seduce stories into inequalities that rouse resentment. Rousseau's chastening of literary strategies is a corrective to an age that has forgotten what his early discourse had affirmed: that arts and sciences "owe their birth to our vices,"[10] but should be able to support civic virtue. When the desire for fame, approbation, and applause deflects the arts from their task of enriching government bodies with knowledge and insight in the service of civilization to the courting of social pleasure, they give us the appearance of virtues, not their cultivation. Rousseau's deepest resentment might be that his own power to rule and to influence is exiled from central seats of power and necessarily confined to the country, the only place, in the present age, where the arts can regain their virtue. The art of pleasing has corrupted even the divine Molière, who, for the sake of aesthetic interest, makes a mockery of Alcèste's high moral standards. If display in the city's theater promotes inequalities in class, sex, talents, if it promotes divorce between appearance and being, then the master of virtue, always at a disadvantage in the world, must not display himself, but must retire to the country. The voice must not be heard. In Paris, "At the heart of the whirlpool" (JJR, *Conf,* 456), Grimm, Baron d'Holbach, Diderot, potentially Rousseau's new family of ideal virtue, betray and divide the world between them; acting together, they "make themselves heard by everybody: great men, wits, men of letters, lawyers, and women" (JJR, *Conf,* 457). Rousseau, on the other hand, wanders into the woods whence he shouts to those in the city "in a feeble voice which they could not hear, 'Madmen who ceaselessly complain of Nature, learn that all your misfortunes arise from yourselves'" (JJR, *Conf,* 362). Without the steady training of his Emile to make commensurate capacity and desire, Rousseau cannot trust himself in the city's labyrinths. But Balzac can, in the skin of a poet, with more desire than willpower, make of incommensurability at once a legitimate field of temptation for the politics of vengeance and a moral testimony to wasted illusions.

10. Rousseau, "A Discourse on the Moral Effects of the Arts and Sciences," 14.

While Balzac, in his novels, delights in the traffic of talent,[11] while he morally censures, associates with actors, is thrilled by spectacular costumes and the wit that, indifferent to virtue, easily avenges exclusion, Rousseau deliberately dresses against fashion at his own opera and, after fantasizing social humiliation, rejects the king's pension. The spectacles that promote "factions, parties, and private vengeances" (JJR, *Ltr,* 121) are censured in the letters of Saint-Preux as well. The desire to be seen, to be heard, to write within the social world carries with it a vulnerability to vengeance, that "guilty and unfortunate passion" (JJR, *Conf,* 464). That is why the writing of *La Nouvelle Héloise* causes him so much shame. Would he entertain the social world, relieve his own passions, traffic himself? If he is not being forced to speak in spite of himself, why must he be hidden in the country (JJR, *Conf,* 263)? The innocent entertainments that democratize sex, age, and rank (JJR, *Ltr,* 125) are not, as Balzac knew, the stuff of novels. The ideal discourse of Balzac's cenacle, mocked by the journalists, serves in his novels as moral foil to the riot of prostitution, to aesthetic pleasures in the palaces of temptation. In Rousseau's *Confessions,* ideal discourse was continually adulterated by the wit and hypocrisy of the Enlightenment illuminati themselves. The writing, then, that is compelled, not merely against misunderstanding, but for the truth, claims an innocence never dreamed of in Balzac's philosophy. (Rousseau himself admits that it was not beyond him to force this design and that it was not uncharacteristic of him to get himself dismissed from the service of a count and his company in order to imagine them in the wrong, justifying himself in his own eyes by claiming that his action had been thrust upon him [R, *Conf,* 100–101].) The writing that Rousseau made antisocial—apostrophe, reverie, letter—pretends to serve society and allows aggression without guilt. Accused by the Genevan consistory of heresies, Rousseau wishes he could force the ministers to *read* his conversation, and wishes his inhibited tongue could have been his pen in the defense of outraged innocence: "With what superiority, with what ease would I have crushed that poor minister. . . . Greed for authority having made the Protestant clergy forget all the principles of the Reformation, all that I needed, to remind him of this and reduce him to silence, was to explain my first *Letters Written from the Mountain* on which they had been so foolish as to censure me" (JJR, *Conf,* 577).

Away from men, Rousseau can easily displace the motive of vengeance by the motive of justice, the need to crush by the need to put things right.

---

11. The reference to Rousseau's formula occurs in a letter of the spoiled poet Lucien in Balzac's *Lost Illusions,* 631; henceforth cited in the text as HB, *Lost.* This is a phrase Rousseau uses to describe the life of actors in JJR, *Ltr,* 79.

When he sees Grimm's disguise of innocence, his expression of justified conduct, Rousseau starts worrying about his own motives. And when he claims that the bad situations of cities too easily protect the guilty, we might suspect that, like Kierkegaard, whom he strongly influenced, he did not have enough trust in his own virtue simultaneously to marry into the world and to keep faith with absolutes. Both were terrified of the demonic aspects of their motives. Both speared the world with their pens and, refusing response, spent a lifetime raising the act to disinterested public service. But Kierkegaard constantly confessed this condition, suspected his motives, and warded off our suspicions of this professional claim: "I, by a concatenation of every sort of evil, was doomed one day to be an example to all who, solely out of a love for justice and the public good, and strong in their innocence alone, might dare openly to speak the truth to men, without relying on cabals or forming parties to protect themselves" (JJR, *Conf,* 214). The recourse to adverbs of exclusion signals Rousseau's fear. Nothing could have seared him more than Diderot's indirect dig that the man who lives apart and alone is wicked (JJR, *Conf,* 423). For he knew his virtue depended on being out of sight of men and their cities.

This nervous and imperious defense provoked a pattern by which the French novelists who followed Rousseau could explore their own passions for revenge. It is hard to disagree with Erich Auerbach that Rousseau's vision was reductively represented in those novels as "the tendency to flee from society, the need to retire and to be alone."[12] When the novelists have recourse in their fiction to the powerful example of Rousseau, we can see how quickly his life and views became allegory. He has written for Stendhal's Julien "the only book his imagination had made use of in constructing a picture of the social world." This impression is not at all altered by the later condescension toward Rousseau by Stendhal's callow hero, who exposes his own feelings of inferiority when he scorns Mathilde's effort to identify him with the antisocial author of *The Confessions.* "In my opinion," Julien declares, "Jean-Jacques Rousseau was nothing but a fool when he undertook to pass judgment on society; he understood it not at all and brought to it the feelings of a flunkey who has risen above his station."[13] Rousseau is to be found in Balzac whenever virtue is signaled by a "simple way of life, . . . frugality, . . . modest requirements," most often to flout the passion for money as a basis for political qualification: "Jean-Jacques Rousseau would not be eligible!" (HB, *Cou,* 418). Again his heroism is associated with his generously unprotected temperament: "the unhappy youth, whose destiny was a little like that of Jean-Jacques Rousseau, imi-

12. "In the Hôtel de la Mole," in *Mimesis,* 466–67.
13. Stendhal, *Red and Black,* 15, 229.

tated him in this respect: he was fascinated by Madame d'Espard and fell in love with her immediately" (HB, *Lost,* 178). This tilter at cities, this enemy of quarrels, this holy fool can even be used as one who, "sublime" and "penniless," was "irresistibly drawn to that radiant centre where men achieve glory through the fervour enkindled in them by the friction of rivalry" (HB, *Lost,* 141).

Rousseau's heroism brings to consciousness the novelist's tortured task of finding structural and stylistic strategies to exonerate while executing vengeance, though his disciples might not realize it. His *advertised* temperament is evident in that of Balzac's cenacle, a correction of the encyclopedist circle, now in the capitol and both great and good, natural, open, unconstrained (HB, *Lost,* 220–23), especially as it is set against the cunning, two-faced, shifty character of Parisian journalists, perpetrators of cabals and strategies of revenge. The "living encyclopaedia of angelic spirits" (HB, *Lost,* 223) holds discussions free of envy, full of passion, immune to social advantage, dedicated to the progress of civilization. Hidden and isolated from the battle plans of Parisian lions and dandies, these saints are Rousseaus of the forest who sing unseen (HB, *Lost,* 191), patiently waiting for a lasting "real" domination of a society they depict as "real" poets of the scene (HB, *Lost,* 510). In the country, doctors like Benassis, healing wounds suffered in the city, follow Rousseau's pattern of authoring social theory from a distance. Rousseau gives prison pastorals and soliloquies to the Stendhalian hero to protect those "lofty virtues and enthusiasms . . . of little use in society" (JJR, *Conf,* 93). To Flaubert, he gave the impulse to distance himself from social seduction so that, by sabotaging Balzac's plots in his bourgeois novels, their ridiculous arrogation of cause and effect, turning them into mere drift or formula, he could keep his genius innocent of the text's bourgeois stupidity. He could avenge it by the debilitating of motive, escape from immersion, and seek in his romances of history (a place like Rousseau's country) sensuously expressive but innocent fulfillment, cruel but not stupid. These styles are modes of vengeance against society's marriages, which exclude the virginal and virtuous poets who tap the full violence of lyrical lands beyond the cheap romance of bourgeois morality.

But the Balzac in love with "bad situations," who, like the best carriers of literary amateurism, eagerly reads his body into his books as a secretary of society and its amorous subverter, will not confine the provincial Rousseau to the garrets of Paris. In the body of Lucien, he exposes him to the spectacular crowds of impressions and expressions, hosts to ambiguous motives, scrambled guilts. The magic ring that grants the novelist both presence and invisibility, prized by Balzac, is feared by a Rousseau we might imagine proleptically nervous about his place in the novel of his boldest disciple, for he knows it would trap him in the social world of the city (JJR, *Rev,* 81–83). All-powerful, he would nevertheless be dependent for his own creations on social material, on plots. And worse, with both social power and impunity, how could vengeful motives ever be separated from the service of truth? The obsessive word of the *Reveries* is *dédommagement,* and, like the *Confessions,* the *Reveries* can be viewed as a place in which retribution becomes innocent. As a country botanist, Rousseau is able to assure himself that no seed of vengeance can grow in his heart and that the best vengeance is that resorted to by the wisest of men: of being happy in spite of one's persecutors. The desire to become well known has died, because to be well known is to be known as guilty and vengeful as well as innocent and generous (JJR, *Rev,* 89–90, 7).

One of the saintly geniuses of *Lost Illusions* is Michel Chréstien, a figure Balzac inherited as a Romantic stereotype and infused with Rousseau's desire for social innocence and virtue. Chréstien pleads with Lucien to put satisfactions of "friendship" over those of "petty requital": "put virtue into your actions and vice into your fictions; instead, as d'Arthez said, of thinking well and behaving badly" (HB, *Lost,* 227). The Rousseau in Balzac recognizes that virtue, acting in the social world, is victimized and mocked. The journalist Etienne Lousteau, as the demonic counterpart of the cenacle advisers, free to seduce Lucien by giving Balzac's view, which would, in Flaubert, suffer the humiliation of unconscious cliché, asks the potential novelist, Lucien:

> Yes, you'll write instead of acting, you'll sing instead of fighting, you'll do your loving, hating and living in the books you write; but when you've saved up your riches for your style, your gold and purple for your characters, when you walk in rags through the streets of Paris, happy to have launched on the world, in rivalry with the Registry Office, a creature named Adolphe, Corinna, Clarissa or Manon, when you've ruined your life and digestion giving birth to this creation, you'll see it slandered, betrayed, sold into slavery, deported to the salt marshes of oblivion by the journalists and committed to the grave by your best friends. Will you be able to wait for the day when your creation will spring to life once more—resurrected by whom, when and how? (HB, *Lost,* 250–51)

Against society's arrogant and active abuse (as opposed to the indifference and pettiness of Flaubert's society, even its vengeance), the genius might use its dearest weapon: journalism. Journalism's strategic acts of exile and exclusion make it a tempting instrument for the artist who, as double agent, could bring society to its knees, and quickly. But because it is so exposed, its wicked and faithless wit heard, given a power refused in Flaubert to work itself free of the authorial satire it appropriates, its changing costumes of party and opinion seen all too well in the social whirlpool of Paris, journalism serves best only as a lightning rod for the novelist's true

and hidden fury against the persecutors of genius; it is valuable as a cor-
rupter of weak talents. It provides the cheap parody of authorial vengeance
against social exclusions, so brilliantly reversed and played out in the open,
that Balzac can stay behind it, in the novel, provisionally released from
traditional bourgeois guilt over expressive power in the public world. He
also finds aesthetic relief under the cover of moral condemnation and in
the melodrama of the subversive criminal (Vautrin) or home-breaker (Bette).
The erotic, social, literary exclusions endured by Balzac, which reinforced a
sense of primary abandonment, vent their rage through these disguises,
which carry the full passion of his genius.

The family betrayal, so obviously felt and avenged in the portrait of
Bette, the sense that his mother hated him, favored a love child, pushed
him out too early, is soothed by Rousseau's trinity, made for souls both
timid and passionate, which grants communion beyond the threatening
rivalry of sex. Before the consummation of his affair with Madame de
Berny, Balzac puts himself into *La Nouvelle Héloïse* and identifies himself
with Claire, as one bearing a noble love rewarded only by its own beauty.[14]
He asks the married Madame de Berny to remember the pure and great
Rousseau, who traced the picture of two ideal women loving the same man.
As Claire, Balzac asserts his sorrows are sweet and he is happy. The divine
trinity of "virtue, love, and nature" that Saint-Preux finds in Julie (JJR,
Nouv, 61) is matched by the union of character, nature, and genius in Balzac's d'Arthez, one of those rare talents rewarded, like Balzac at the end
of his stint as rival to the Registry Office, with the trinity of genius,
woman, and wealth of rank. This triangular ideal is, precisely, a counterexclusion that bypasses social approval, does not seem to need it. If it stays
in the world, it is oblivious of social advantage. But Balzac, lover of plots,
wanted to infiltrate that society in his novels, both to enjoy it and to forge
an ingenuous vengeance by strategic subversion. The motives are consubstantial as he undoes Rousseau's arduous work of purification, refusing the
defense of historical drift against the will. By *his* depiction of historical
confusion, Flaubert punishes bourgeois desire for purpose and excuse,
forcing Providence to flutter as its mere rhetorical ghost: empty fate. He
reminds us why even the weak of character never drift in the novels of
Balzac.

That novelist settles into the skin of his hero Lucien, experiences the
position of a pariah excluded from the aristocracy of provincial Angoulême
before entry into Madame de Bargeton's salon, where his promise is both
recognized and mocked by the jealous fops. Lucien's patroness continually
reminds him that society takes its revenge for any happiness it does not

14. Balzac to Madame de Berny, October 4, 1822, *Correspondance de Balzac,* 1:208.

share, and she indicates the way in which the genius can effect a counter-vengeance; he can, for example, make up for his lowly position by the "disdainful eye" he casts on the world (HB, *Lost,* 27). Lucien comes to believe that, sooner or later, the "genius in him [will] shine forth like that of so many men, his predecessors, who had brought society to heel" (HB, *Lost,* 63). The vision of Paris stimulates in him the thought that is characteristic of those Balzac heroes who are more ambitious than fine in character: "So that is my kingdom! . . . That is the society I have to tame" (HB, *Lost,* 182). Even Lucien's rival and social superior, du Châtelet, wanting the social field for himself, advises him that there is compensation for social abandonment: "You are a man of genius: see if you can't avenge yourself. Society disdains you: disdain society. Take refuge in a garret, write masterpieces, acquire some sort of prestige and you will have society at your feet. Then you will pay it back for the wounds it inflicted on you here in Paris" (HB, *Lost,* 186). Once again, we have a perverted carrier of d'Arthez's words, for du Châtelet is only too happy to hoist the genius on the social hook.

What is of interest here is what all readers drawn into Balzac's world have noticed as his major strength, that the novelist married his desire to free his genius from and saturate it in society's bad situations because, as Henry James insisted, social saturation in his life became the sign of his authenticity in his literature. (To Marxist readers, it enabled him to reveal a larger politics than the one he professed.) Lucien's brother-in-law, David, a genius of the provinces, carries out Rousseau's dream. Hidden, hounded by persecutors, he gives up his art to establish a bourgeois household, but not before furthering civilization by his inventions for which he is not credited. He is clearly Rousseau's provincial giant of natural and unaffected talent and imagination who humiliates the scornful Parisian wits by leaving legacies of discoveries, useful inventions (JJR, *Ltr,* 59–60). But he is not the stuff of interesting novels. The plots of his creditors most certainly are. How can Balzac's liberated passion stay with the prostitution of the city, compete for power with its flamboyant magnetism, when he acknowledges that Rousseau's analysis of Parisian circles, exposed in *The Confessions* and *La Nouvelle Héloise,* was a moral indictment that had to be honored? If social participation is both delight and entrapment, if it brings the necessary knowledge for subversion to the exiled and anarchic novelists, it brings as reward the means to turn away hounding creditors and to outwit unscrupulous journalists and publishers whose own vengeance condemns itself while their author enjoys vicarious persecuting. Only spasmodically does the novelist dally in the plotless garrets and provinces of genius to remind us that virtue has a future.

This double action is vividly spotted by Vautrin. Disguised as a priest, he warns Lucien that suicide is homage to society, a cooperative self-exclusion.

If the individual wants to reassume his power, arrogated by the world, he must begin "by obeying society and studying it closely" (HB, *Lost,* 642). How can he wisely study the society that perpetually stirs in him desires of vengeance? "Was Lucien arousing some regret in Madame de Bargeton's heart? His mind was preoccupied with this thought: at the sight of the Corinna of Angoulême a desire for vengeance stirred his heart as on the day when, in the Champs-Elysées, she and her cousin had treated him with contempt" (HB, *Lost,* 369). How can one both feel and study this desire, penetrate it and rise above it? Often Balzac speaks of the dual nature, analyzed by Freud, of our desire for ideal love and pleasure. As a novelist, he identifies himself with his Baron Hulot, whose quest for happiness ends "in two volumes," the love of energetic vice and the worship of passive virtue (HB, *Cou,* 288–89). The novel's melodrama manifests this strain. He also identifies himself with the rare woman who has genius enough to satisfy both spiritual love and sex. If this double nature can live comfortably in one body, it might be in that of the novelist who has the "gift of such paradoxical yet superb abilities" (HB, *Cou,* 299). Great novelists court and house courtesans and wives. But as true lovers, they are also like eunuchs (HB, *Cou,* 397), immune to the seductions of the world they exhaust. In this solitary and divine form, the novelist knows vengeance is his, for this is a body married only to its creation. How to unite the force that feeds at "the breast of a woman with the force of God?"[15] By becoming, in his novel, not the Janus of secular secretaries, but triangular, like an amateur God (HB, *Lost,* 372–73), resistant to the neutralizing impulse of Rousseau's ménage à trois with fathers, mothers, sisters, rivals.

To persuade Lucien to prostitute his principles, the cynical journalist Blondet claims that great thoughts are bilateral and great writers are masters of alternation (HB, *Lost,* 372–73), but Balzac subscribes to this conceit only with those parts of the novelist that serve as secretary, with the curiosity and cunning of a concierge, and as poet of his characters. Blondet's Alceste says "yes," his Philinte "no," but Balzac's Molière is great because he holds them together as conflict, not contradiction. The novelist can and must, after all, put opinions in different mouths, and we have already seen how fully Balzac bent his master thoughts to suit the speaker. We are "great relativists," claims Blondet (HB, *Lost,* 373); and the Balzac who announces himself in the famous "Avant-Propos" to *La Comédie humaine* as an anatomist of the *facts* of passion, of types, of vices and virtues—*that* Balzac puts the search for the absolute in its social place. But Balzac's novelist is more than that; as comfortable, unlike Rousseau, with the magic ring as with a complex Molière, he assumes the

---

15. These lines are in the last paragraph of Balzac's novel *Le Curé de Tours.*

power of the invisible deity. In fact, Balzac projects himself, in the novels, as triangular, as he forces a rich competition between the secretary who can depict manners and preach morality with full social and political integrity (family, monarchy, Catholicism), the strong poet of character who can enter skins, and the anarchist subverter of the social world, the energetic avenger of exclusion whose social innocence is periodically ransomed by the secretary. The secretary might resolve, through the mind of Victorin, "to make the best of his Celestine, although she was certainly not the wife he had dreamed of," and thus might achieve "a balanced view of life," through the realization that "we are obliged by the universal law to be content with a more or less imperfect approximation to the ideal" (HB, *Cou,* 348). Or he might revise Rousseau in the "Avant-Propos" and maintain that man is neither good nor bad, that society, far from perverting him, renders him better, though it offers to his interests those irresistible plots of bad situations that can turn him away from virtue. While the secretary of society is fascinated by architecture as a sign, code, and fossil of a whole culture, he is made triangular by a vision that goes beyond that of the miller and his wife who gaze upon the sleeping and defeated Lucien: "Neither the miller nor his wife had any idea that, besides actors, princes and bishops, there exists a kind of man who is both prince and actor, a man who discharges a splendid sacerdotal function: the Poet, who seems to be doing nothing but nevertheless reigns over Humanity once he has learnt how to depict it" (HB, *Lost,* 481). This is the power of the invisible ring, which is not ashamed to couple the novelist with Rousseau's despised actors, or with priests, or even with thieves, who depend upon the social world but rise above it by their alliance with the large passions of nature. The identity of novelist and thief is a stunning violation of Rousseau's quarantining of ethics from plots, but it puts in provisional play the innocence of his revenge:

A thief is a rare man. He is nature's spoiled child. She has heaped upon him all sorts of perfections: an imperturbable sang-froid, unfailing daring, the art of seizing the occasion . . . nimbleness, courage, a good constitution, piercing eyes, agile hands, a happy and expressive face. All these advantages are nothing special for a thief, yet they already form the sum of talents of a Hannibal, a Catiline, a Marius, a Caesar.

Is it not necessary, in addition, that the thief know men, their character and their passions? that he lie smoothly, foresee events, judge the future, have a fine and quick mind? that he have a lively understanding, be a good actor and mime? that he be able to seize the tone and manners of the various classes of society, ape the clerk, the banker, the general, know their habits, and clothe himself at need in the toga of the police prefect or the yellow trousers of the policeman? Finally—most difficult and wonderful of all, the advantage that gives the Homers, Ariostos, tragic authors, and comic poets their renown—must he not have imagination, brilliant, divine imagination? Must he not be perpetually inventing new plots? For him to be booed means to go to the galleys.[16]

So here is Balzac, the triangular genius, married both to society and to his own creation.

Balzac, in the midst of his plots and characters, is the secret spy (one of his favorite epithets for the novelist), the Vautrin who calls himself a student of Rousseau in *Le Père Goriot,* because he protests against the profound deceptions of the social contract by an undemocratic world of exclusions. Through Bette and Vautrin, Balzac's vengeance makes sociable Rousseau's divorce from society with his own marriage to it, as they plot, prime, and propel their darling dandies and bourgeois courtesans to power and defeat. Like Balzac, the latter use society's own weapons of persecution with the delight of one included who, nevertheless, stands in a position of powerful exile. Is there much distance between Balzac and Vautrin when the novelist revels in the whole game of seeing and being viewed in theaters (that staple of the novel), so thoroughly explored by Rousseau, who, in his fiercest indictment against the lure of the spectacular, asks us to imagine a theater at the summit of the mountain of his folk society (JJR, *Ltr,* 62–64)? Eyes and costumes are agents and objects of mutual enchantment and disenchantment for those who play this game. That is why Balzac, as a strong poet, needs "to get into [Lucien's] skin and study the mechanism of feeling" (HB, *Lost,* 412). His conductor sees Lucien seeing, but, as a weak poet, not properly studying himself and his rivals at the Tuileries, lacking the moral sense that should accompany observation: "So then we see Lucien in high feather, with springy gait, treading on air, emerging on to the Terrasse des Feuillants, striding through it and studying the people walking along it: pretty women with their admirers, elegant couples arm in arm, greeting one another with a glance as they passed by. . . . How much finer than those of Angoulême were the birds on this magnificent perch! It was like the riot of colour blazing forth on ornithological species from India or America compared with the drab plumage of European birds. Lucien . . . angrily took stock of his own appearance and condemned it" (HB, *Lost,* 164). Now, together, they gaze at Coralie: "Coralie was the joy of the audience: all eyes were spanning her waist in its close-fitting basquine, caressing her Andalusion curves and the sensual undulations their movement transmitted to her skirt" (HB, *Lost,* 295). Later in the novel, she accompanies Lucien and helps him take the short and unearned revenge of the social genius, who helps us to lose interest in moral choice by charging an alliance of politics and aesthetics: "In one of the lanes of the Bois de

16. "Code des gens honnêtes," in *Oeuvres de H. de Balzac,* 21:6. This is my translation.

Boulogne their coupe encountered the barouche of Mesdames d'Espard and de Bargeton who gazed at Lucien with astonishment: he darted at them the contemptuous glance of a poet who foresees the fame in store for him and intends to exploit his power. The instant when a single glare directed at these two women enabled him to convey some of the vengeful thoughts which, thanks to them, were gnawing at his heart, was one of the sweetest moments in his life, and perhaps decided his destiny" (HB, *Lost,* 326). Probably this scene was in the mind of Proust when he has Marcel return, toward the end of his novel, to the Bois de Boulogne where, once, the beautiful women were goddesses to him. The future novelist will find his vengeance for betrayal by investing divine belief no longer in their beauty and social desirability, but in his authorship. But Vautrin, as agent for Balzac's authorship, will not be released into the solitude of the study. At any rate, this scene in Balzac corroborates Rousseau's contention that vengeance feeds upon the spectacular, upon the rivalries of seeing. And the courtesan Josépha echoes Rousseau when she admits that she belongs to Art while the saintly Baroness Hulot belongs to Virtue (HB, *Cou,* 371). But without recourse to courtesans, Balzac cannot achieve his victory. Balzac's power and his cunning enable him to cross those thresholds of our worst desires, and survive. His participations earn the vengeance that is beyond good and evil. Claude Vignon assures his fellow journalists that a common attack will be like a firing squad. All shall be innocent of the hits (HB, *Lost,* 314). By splitting his vision, Balzac gains vengeance against all the exclusions that fed his gigantic energies, and he does it by using himself freely, giving up some of his strength to his mistresses, to the journalists, and by enjoying the surprises of his purgatory of plot where art and the social world are equal and inseparable powers.

His great admirer, Proust, reduces Balzac to a dualist as he spots, like so many others, the vulgarity that marked his praise of virtue. His ideal, Proust claims, was to "get on in the world virtuously and in a Christian spirit; for Balzac knew he ought to paint a saintly figure, but he could not conceive how social success should not be the goal of all goals, even in the eyes of a saint."[17] We know how much it bothered Proust that Balzac put "the achievements of life and literature on exactly the same level" (MP, *Art,* 159). So it is touchingly ironic that Proust defends him against his enemy Sainte-Beuve, who would do the same, and starts by acknowledging that "even in those of us whom highmindedness specifically impels to reject vulgar motives, to condemn and disinfect them, those motives may exist, fundamental though transfigured" (MP, *Art,* 160). The fundamental mo-

---

17. "Contre Sainte-Beuve," in *Marcel Proust on Art and Literature, 1896–1919,* 158; henceforth cited in the text as MP, *Art.*

tives mapped by Rousseau have been transfigured from novelist to novelist, and Proust's novel clearly partakes of that legacy. Out of Rousseau's hatred for confusions between appearance and being comes Proust's professional protest against Sainte-Beuve's failure to see "the gulf that separates the writer from the man of the world"; but the legacy suffers an ironic twist, for Rousseau, dedicated not to consubstantiality but to identity, would have hated the salvaging of the writer's art by the claim that "the writer's true self is manifested only in his books" (MP, *Art,* 106). *En revanche,* Rousseau was such a fine student of the terrible metamorphoses of his own character in the Parisian coteries marked by inequality, exclusive codes of wit, that he helped to pay for Proust's retreat to the innocence of his study (a far cry from Montaigne's porous den) and allowed him to make the terrible split between the man in the salon and the man in his cork-lined room a principal design of his book. Sainte-Beuve's motive was one Rousseau anticipated as inevitable for the social artist, the applause of the social world:

> What one bestows on private life—in conversation, that is, however refined it may be (and the most refined is the worst, since it falsifies the life of the mind by getting it mixed up in it: Flaubert's conversations with his niece and the clockmaker had no harm in them) or in those drawing-room essays, whittled down to suit a particular circle and scarcely more than conversation in print—is the product of a quite superficial self, not of the innermost self which one can only recover by putting aside the world and the self that frequents the world; that innermost self which has waited while one was in company, which one feels certain is the only real self, and which artists—and they only—end by living for, like a god whom they less and less often depart from, and to whom they have sacrificed a life that has no purpose except to do him honour. (MP, *Art,* 104)

Proust's deepest self masterfully exploits this confusion as a defense against the dreaded motive of revenge.

In a remarkable letter about the Dreyfus case, Proust reflected in 1906:

> Alas, in the last ten years, we have all had many a sorrow, many a disappointment, many a torment in our lives. And not for one of us will the hour strike that will change our sorrows into exaltation, our disappointments into fulfillment, and our torment into exquisite triumphs. I shall become more and more ill, more and more I shall miss the ones I have lost, and all that I dreamed of in my life will be farther and farther beyond my reach. But for Dreyfus and for Picquart it is not so. For them life has been "providential" after the fashion of fairy tales and serial thrillers. That is because our suffering was founded on fact—on truths—physiological truths, human and emotional truths. For them, suffering was founded on error. Fortunate, indeed, are those who are victims of

error—judicial or otherwise! They are the only human beings for whom there are redress and restitution.[18]

If we feel the powerful desire for redress and retribution bucking against the slow and patient unfolding of consciousness in *Remembrance of Things Past,* is it not because Proust tried to find a way to change his existential torment into exquisite triumph, to gain judicial retribution for the ontological flaw? Marcel sees Dostoyevsky's novels as a long frieze on which the tale of vengeance and expiation is continually displayed, and I would like to suggest that Proust, too, paints murals of his vengeance against sorrows and disappointment, and of his expiation. Despite his generous inclusion of the reader in his plaint of impotent suffering from truths, Proust makes us hostages to his creative will, for we are all parents, Swanns, Verdurins, Albertines, Sainte-Beuves, all perpetrators of false marriages, of primal unions that yield up their exclusive authority to the child's pleas. Like his characters, as mere amateurs of style and friendship who sap the virgin energy of high art, we need to be punished by parody, especially when we carelessly identify the public with the private novelist. Not for Proust the consubstantiality of justice and grace in and between marriage, a dinner party, a painting Woolf puts in play in *To the Lighthouse.* He seems drawn to us because our desires as social identities must be appealing, if demonic, decoys for the artist rising slowly to his exquisite triumph: "But when a belief vanishes, there survives it—more and more vigorously so as to cloak the absence of the power, now lost to us, of imparting reality to new things—a fetishistic attachment to the old things which it did once animate, as if it was in them and not in ourselves that the divine spark resided, and as if our present incredulity had a contingent cause—the death of the gods."[19]

The passage from the child's providence to the artist's will suffers successive social entrances and disillusions. If the will spends itself in this mock, merely professional purgatory marked by the double desire to worship and violate, yield and conquer, if, in its youngest stages, it imagines, as Marcel later claims, parental plots against which it can test its rebellious and persuasive powers (MP, *Rem,* 3:666), if, like Rousseau's, it knows that the kiss of Maman is both a victory and a defeat, if it endures salons, friendships, reading continually marked by the rhythm of belief and betrayal, is not the marriage dreamed up by Balzac, between the great man and his creation, fully justified and purified? Does not the ascent to this marriage achieve a judiciary redress for the inequality between Providence

---

18. Proust to Mme Straus, after July 13, 1906, *Letters of Marcel Proust,* 153.

19. Marcel Proust, *Remembrance of Things Past,* 1:460; henceforth cited in the text as MP, *Rem.*

and the personal will? The necessary agony of holding Albertine captive pays for this question: "Could life console me for the loss of art? Was there in art a more profound reality, in which our true personality finds an expression that is not afforded it by the activities of life?" (MP, *Rem,* 3:155). Art triumphs over the torment of the child's exclusion and counterexclusion. As an agent of the will, it hides its aggression behind memory and association, sending out as scapegoats demonic distortions of its own true forms, false starts, false styles, false theories. The vision of art achieved at the end of the novel blends the desires of the parent and child in an innocent marriage of belief and will because it has been professionally patient through parody, satire, lyric ups and downs.

Like Kafka, Proust senses that, since writing is rebellion against the father, it is a psychological source of torment. When Marcel's mother accepts Albertine only if she can make him happy, Marcel realizes:

> But by these very words which left it to me to decide my own happiness, my mother had plunged me into that state of doubt in which I had been plunged long ago when, my father having allowed me to go to *Phèdre* and, what was more, to take up writing as a career, I had suddenly felt myself burdened with too great a responsibility, the fear of distressing him, and that melancholy which we feel when we cease to obey orders which, from one day to another, keep the future hidden, and realise that we have at last begun to live in real earnest, as a grown-up person, the life, the only life that any of us has at his disposal. (MP, *Rem,* 2:958–59)

But if the father's permission for art stimulates stirrings of will in the child to avenge himself against generosity, it also starts the purgatorial journey that leads to the marriage of the artist only with his creation. That marriage triumphs over paternal permission by a gradual and apparently innocent discovery of the relentless analogies between the marriages that tease the expressive will into a social wasteland: "I wondered whether marriage with Albertine might not spoil my life, not only by making me assume the too arduous task of devoting myself to another person, but by forcing me to live apart from myself because of her continual presence and depriving me forever of the joys of solitude" (MP, *Rem,* 3:19–20). Art is excused for consuming its content, the long and repetitive experience of others, and, as in Flaubert's *Sentimental Education,* a great model for Proust's novel, for killing by analogy, to avenge, as the amateur Kafka never will in his plots, the world's persistent betrayal of being. It is the cruel, but innocent, law of art that human beings must die so that it may prosper by its mastery not only of Time, but of the ambivalent struggle between belief and will. The novelist depicts the social world necessarily subverted by secret homosexual impasses because art must become the only bride with whom he can live in consecrated freedom from those wars of exclusion and counterexclusion that are the symptoms of our inability to change sorrows into exaltation, disappointments into fulfillments, torment into exquisite triumphs. Like Proust, both Rousseau and Balzac imagined that to live in the social world was to live in a house in which we are victimized by servants who take advantage of our needs. Their ruses and demands plot by the obligatory social betrayals that justify the aggressive wish for revenge: "It is hard to imagine how much pestering genuine grief has to endure from legal formalities. It makes civilization hateful and the customs of savages preferable."[20] In a well-known passage taken over by Shakespeare, Montaigne praises the "savage" society that seems barbarous to Paris: "This is a nation, I should say to Plato, in which there is no sort of traffic, no knowledge of letters, no science of numbers, no name for a magistrate or for political superiority, no custom of servitude, no riches or poverty, no contracts, no successions, no partitions, no occupations but leisure ones, no care for any but common kinship, no clothes, no agriculture, no metal, no use of wine or wheat. The very words that signify lying, treachery, dissimulation, avarice, envy, belittling, pardon—unheard of" (M, 1:31.153). Yet he makes cannibalism only consubstantial with Parisian civilization. For neither Montaigne nor Balzac would change his conditions: they are French, they are Catholics, and they are among the greatest literary carriers of amateurism.

20. Honoré de Balzac, *Cousin Pons,* 285–86.

5

THE DOCTOR IN SPITE OF HIMSELF

The Prescriptions of Zeno

Le Médecin malgré lui.

Molière

When we hear the irresistible Zeno, impelled by so many mixed motives, launch his climactic, witty insight, "Life is neither good nor bad; it is original,"[1] we recognize his power to characterize our experience of modern life, which can neither do without nor be contained by the bourgeois desire to be good. But the adage also serves to caricature the now notorious contemporary reaction to Svevo's fiction. Reviewers of his first two novels, and even of his masterpiece, *Confessions of Zeno,* tended to denigrate the Triestine writer as, rather than good or bad, merely original. That is why, when James Joyce introduced him to an appreciative European circle in Paris as a novelist who was not only original but astonishingly good, Svevo, lacking the confidence in his genius that carried Joyce through so much frustration, was amazed. Calling himself, in the face of his belated fame, a "bambino di 64 anni,"[2] he charmed his hosts at a 1928 Paris literary dinner in his honor by filtering his ingenuous joy through a screen of cigarette smoke. He was even more amazed to discover, as the young poet Eugenio Montale championed his cause in Italy, that he was being hailed as the revolutionary father of a new generation of Italian writers.

Though the years of Svevo's literary production correspond to the con-

---

1. Italo Svevo, *Confessions of Zeno,* 299; henceforth cited in the text as IS, *Zeno.*
2. Svevo to Valéry Larbaud, September 15, 1925, *Opera omnia,* 1:764. Translations from letters, notebooks, diaries, and Italian critics are mine.

ventional boundaries of modernism, 1880–1928, the novelist, repeatedly charged by Italian critics with an anti-literary adulteration of his syntax, diction, and rhythms, thought of himself as behind the times. In reality, it became clear by the end of his life that his so-called deficiencies had put him ahead of his time and into the company of the greatest international giants of the fiction of his day: Proust, Mann, Kafka, and Joyce. Perhaps to keep from dealing with a disturbingly new scene and subject, professional Italian readers found it hard to get past the formal problem. Svevo was not the first Italian writer, nor would he be the last, to attract the complaints of Academy purists who flinched at a prose tainted by Triestine dialect, but his case, so dramatically publicized, served as a crucial transition to modernity. G. B. Angioletti's confession, in the special 1929 Svevo issue of *Solaria,* exemplifies the nature of the Italian resistance: "It wasn't easy for me to approach Svevo's art: an art far from what was natural to my tastes, an art that did not take into account certain laws of style, certain sacrifices and subtleties that, perhaps wrongly, are dear to me." Svevo, himself, to anticipate and blunt criticism, continually poked fun at his style, even wryly supporting the suggestion that he was famous in Europe because he sounded better in translation. As late as 1925, he could quip, "Now there is no time to straighten out my crooked legs."[3]

In this novel, Zeno's witty deflection of the envy he feels for his brother-in-law Guido, who courts the beautiful Ada in fluent Tuscan, doubles as defense against another rival, the psychoanalyst Dr. S., whose diagnoses threaten to make of Zeno a national case history: "My God! He has only studied medicine, and so he has no idea what writing in Italian means to us who talk dialect but cannot express ourselves in writing. A written confession is always mendacious. We lie with every word we speak in the Tuscan tongue!" (IS, *Zeno,* 368). When he has Zeno mischievously narrow the common post-Romantic anxiety over the truth of confession to a vernacular problem, Svevo is clearly mocking the provincialism that refuses to read past diction.

Gradually, the perpetrator of parochial barbarisms was certified a national treasure. Svevo's new rhythms and awkward syntax, his playful revising, by chapter headings, of sacramental order, led by the smoking problem, proved ideal conductors of an obsessively anxious and hyperconscious modern temperament with its provisional and explosive confessions and corrections, rationalizations and sublimations, sarcasms and self-ironies. A diction vulnerable to mendacities was one that could mix, like the

3. G. B. Angioletti, "Svevo," *Solaria* special issue, 11; see also Piero Gadda, "Lettura di *Senilità,"* in the same issue, 42; Svevo to Giuseppe Prezzolini, November 12, 1925, *Opera,* 1:769.

metaphors of Freud, the voices of bourgeois business and psychology, so often competitive in the fiction of other modern masters. The new hybrid finds a sponsor in Montale: "The men and women of Svevo speak the language of the Tergesteo, the language of old Triestine merchants; this is the music—together with the incessant 'bora'—that underlines the sombre *cafard,* the assiduous inner monologue, the courageous self-auscultation of his characters."[4] The delayed appreciation in Italy, fabled in Svevo's late short story "The Mother," of the "new music," derived from a deferred Italian middle-class life and literature that elsewhere, in the Austro-Hungarian Empire, carried Svevian tones of a nervous and hypochondriacal irony and analysis. A long tradition of literary idealism, of a Catholicism utterly resistant to the alliance, in their mutual suspicion of neutral language, of Marx and Freud, turned a deaf ear to this new composition that orchestrated a rich atmosphere of indeterminism continually qualifying an overdetermining decadence, described by Pirandello as modern inanity: an impotent and bored egoism, an easy pessimism, an exhausted morality and courage, weakness of will, and character kept going by a perpetual recourse to lies.[5]

The groundwork for the appeal to European patrons of *Confessions of Zeno* was secured by an extended post-Romantic literary history of French dandies and drifters doomed to live out bourgeois monarchies, of Slavic superfluous, underground confessors of bad faith, continually insulted and injured, of guilty artist sons of commercial bourgeois fathers in the Austro-Hungarian Empire, sons marked by the self-irony and analytic astuteness of a culture rich in Jewish guilt and humor and drawn to Freud's designs and insights. That culture had been nurtured by Freud's feeders: Schopenhauer, Darwin, and Nietzsche. As a young bank clerk in Trieste, Ettore Schmitz, with a pen name of Italo Svevo (Italian-Swabian) that reflected both his genealogical background and the historical situation of his native city, a mercantile port at once parochial and cosmopolitan, with an Austrian head and an irredentist Italian heart, spent his spare time in the library continuing the reading of continental, English, and Slavic literature and philosophy begun in a German commercial academy in Segnitz-am-Main, where his father had sent him to become a good businessman. Svevo absorbed these depictions and analyses of our humiliating psychological and biological determinisms for use in his novels and found in them a cover for his sense of inferiority and for depression triggered by so many disappointed hopes: a father's commercial bullying and virtual bankruptcy,

4. Eugenio Montale, "Il vento è mutato," *Lettere Italo Svevo: con gli scritti di Montale su Svevo,* 139.
5. Luigi Pirandello, "Arte e coscienza d'oggi," in *Opere,* 6:901–2.

multiple family deaths, his literary neglect. But it was not until the third novel that he could find a tone by which he could both protect his temperament and stimulate his best energies, the double duty defined as health by William James and Freud. Appearing after twenty years of publishing silence (in response, Svevo claimed, to the eloquent and discreet silence of his reviewers),[6] *Confessions of Zeno* radiated an atmosphere so confident of its originality that it could host, without anxiety, all the reading that had formerly inhibited both the novelist and his fictional heroes. The promotion of humor, to liberate the will paralyzed by man's demotion to planetary insignificance, was actually a legacy latent in the perspective of the great dissectors of civilization and its discontents.

Schopenhauer had shown Svevo a way to detach the individual's will and desire from the general push and shove of Nature, interested only in her plans for the species, and sometimes not even in that. He was drawn to the philosopher's cruelly sketched anatomy of the origins of guilts, anxieties, the fear of death, insignificance, dependence. And he was attracted to Schopenhauer's imagination of human life as some kind of cosmic mistake, a considerable blow to the Christian elevation of man above the beasts who, after all, needed no compensatory philosophical systems to make them feel important. It prepared the way for the Darwinian deflation eagerly exploited by Svevo's fables and fictions and by those of writers Svevo came to admire, particularly Strindberg and Kafka. Nietzsche, badly edited, gave Svevo the image of the superman he mocked in the historical form of D'Annunzio and Mussolini, but the novelist was able to learn from him, as from Freud, the many uses of sickness, some honest enough to forge a new heroism of acknowledged ambivalence. He profited from their interest in the repressions and displacements of aggressive instincts, the neuroses of a competitive herd vulnerable to extinction.

But it was the agency of humor that enabled Freud to spin sickness, defenses, and defeats into a more intimate bourgeois sociability, and Schopenhauer, to spiral us up to an aesthetic distance from which we could change the tragedy of man, confident he is being pulled from the front by progressive ideals, to the comedy of man unconscious of being pushed from behind by the will of nature. Mother Nature, the presiding deity of Svevo's authentically original universe, manages to reroute Zeno's desires, by happy mistakes, in the darkness of a séance, to take the right woman: "Who could have foreseen it, that day I went limping from Ada to Alberta to arrive at last at Augusta? I discovered that far from being a blind beast driven by another's will, I was a very clever man" (IS, *Zeno,* 140). Svevo could not utilize the high aesthetic and antisocial slant of Schopenhauer's temper,

6. "Profilo autobiografico," *Opera,* 3:805.

traits the philosopher associated with genius. But he could adopt Freud's trick of temperament—promoting bourgeois order while exploding it. Scenes called Freudian because they revel in humorous slips that can lead Zeno to show up at the wrong funeral are most telling not as they expose guilt but as they serve sociability.

In a late essay, building on earlier ones that Svevo would have read, Freud touchingly pictures humor as the greatest gift granted to the isolated and guilt-ridden ego by the exacting parent, the superego.[7] The gift is bestowed on Zeno throughout his novel. It is bestowed as well, by extension, on his society, which profits so enormously from Zeno's talent for turning funerals into weddings. Like Freud's artist, who serves to organize and express latent desires, frustrations, hostilities for his society as he relieves himself, Zeno overcomes the conflicts evoked by his jealousy of Guido with a magically amusing chatter. In a pivotal scene, he teases the serious guilt of his secret adultery, the serious rivalry with Guido, into an atmosphere that protects both himself and his circle. He claims that the dead Copler is still alive. Later, at the wedding party for Ada and Guido, to extenuate his bad behavior to his father-in-law, Zeno professes to be upset because, in fact, Copler is dead. The laughter of disbelief becomes a reproof that triggers yet another Zeno reversal: "I've caught you! He is still alive and getting better." This juggling act is retrospectively elevated into a comic family legend, and all false reports of deaths are crowned, "like poor Copler" (IS, *Zeno,* 204–5, 210). It is Augusta, one of literature's great wives, who eases the postantic depression of Zeno by assuring him he has changed gloom into joy. Her tender smiles invariably work on Zeno, even in absurd contretemps, as grace. It is she who prizes his confession's sociability over its truth because his lies authenticate their intimacy (IS, *Zeno,* 75). Zeno later uses this precise defense against the psychoanalyst whose authority is conceded, but who needs more practice in reading truths through temperament.

I know of no other major novel that measures morality by the laugh meter. Augusta's superiority to the prettier and sexually more desirable Ada rests on her readiness to laugh; Zeno's to the apparently more manly Guido, on his readiness to joke—gifts almost absent in their competitors. While Zeno envies Augusta's health, located in the undivided consciousness she shares with his father, which feels the earth "motionless and solid, poised between its poles" (IS, *Zeno,* 30), his sickness is continually palliated by her appreciation for the comedy he perpetrates. She senses that, in the end, it will be used conservatively by Mother Nature to make him the best husband in the family (IS, *Zeno,* 312).

7. Sigmund Freud, "Humor," in *The Standard Edition of Complete Psychological Works of Sigmund Freud,* 21:163–166.

With other both culturally marginal and international Austro-Hungarian writers like Kafka, Svevo, suspicious of the therapeutic pretensions of psychoanalysis, was still eager to embrace its insights. One of them motivates a majority of the great scenes in the novel: "It might be said that we owe the fairest flowering of our love to the reaction against the hostile impulse which we sense within us."[8] It is Zeno's humor, converting mixed motives from moral liabilities to moral catalysts, that regulates the psychic economy of the bourgeois "stock market." It refuses to bankrupt any potential speculative material by selling it out and holds open for us a life that suffers its fluctuations between parlors and planets, a life wide with surprise and wonder, if also deep with pain. By making of isolating diagnostic edicts (the undeniable evidence, for example, of an Oedipus complex) a spur to improvisations, Zeno socializes them into shared family romances. While Dr. S. is limited to Freud's tendentious wit, Zeno, using humor as a double agent of defense and mediation, not only rescues his desires from moral and psychological liquidation but liberates as well those of the company around him.

Throughout his adult life, Svevo's humor turned what he fancied as an evolutionary weakness of his temperament into a social strength and made it his, and Zeno's, most cherished and affirmative philosophy of life: amateurism. In an epistolary diary entry of 1896, he assures his fiancée of his aversion to domination, a prime professional urge: "I'm not good for conquering anything. I don't want to conquer anything. I want to have and to hold without force. Otherwise, life becomes disagreeable for me, full of responsibility and threats. If I cannot have and hold without force, I renounce voluntarily." Reconciling his doubts over his coming marriage, Svevo speaks of his temperamental talent for overcoming his chronic jealousy, a crucial strength for a novelist: "It was a major quality of my character up to now to allow to the characters and dispositions around me the full freedom to develop and display themselves according to their own nature. Any interference on my part in these exhibitions would have seemed to me a crime."[9] That quality enables Zeno to elicit from the equivocal origins of *his* marriage a persuasive Svevian truth: "uncertainty has never left me during the whole of my life, and today I am compelled to believe that true love is compatible with such a doubt" (IS, *Zeno,* 127). Svevo fancies, in life and in Zeno, that the dilettantism of his organic development is a result not of that Christian politics of the weak Nietzsche targeted but of a refusal both to dominate and to be dominated (not without qualms and envy) by doc-

8. Freud, "Our Attitude towards Death," in *Works,* 23:299.
9. "Diario per la fidanzata," January 16, 1896, *Opera,* 3:776; "Diario," February 8, 1896, *Opera,* 3:785.

trinal fathers, systems, professions, philosophies: "I think the animal most capable of evolving is the one in whom one part is in continual struggle with another for supremacy, the animal, now or in future generations, who has preserved the possibility of evolving from one part or another in response to what is demanded of it by society, whose needs no one can now foresee. In my absolute lack of any marked development in whatever direction, I am that man. I feel it so strongly that in my solitude I glory in it and I wait, knowing I am nothing but a sketch." Certainly, the sense of being unfinished allows his temperament the protection it needs: "I was healthy, or, at least, I loved my sickness (if sickness it is) enough to want to protect myself thoroughly in the spirit of self defense."[10]

But this decision to live as a psychological, physical, literary, political, ideological amateur, which might have its origin in the fear of death, stoked by a consciousness of ambitious and guilty wishes for the deaths of rivals, sensations of not loving wisely or well, enables a conversion of potentially paralyzing self-pity and reproach into a fruitful social energy. From Montaigne, Svevo might have learned that Death has a hard time finding an amateur, and from Freud that history has a hard time humiliating a writer who only daydreams. A mock competition between the artist and the businessman as daydreamer protects Svevo's resentment of dependency on the profitable marine-paint company of his wife's family and his disappointment at his failure to achieve fame as a writer: "You know that in spite of my serious effort to become in the shortest possible time a good businessman and a good industrialist, in fact I have only the intention. I remain in the face of the new purpose the old dreamer. When I foresee a piece of business, I at least have had the practical sense to think and dream of it in the forms and terms in which it presents itself. Oh, I go so far into it that the business itself soon becomes a misfortune but the stimulation for dreams so powerful as to procure me a distraction that some day will topple me into a paint basin."[11] But behind the screen of amateurism, he became, in fact, both a good industrialist and an original writer.

The long years between his second novel and *Confessions of Zeno,* years in which Svevo pretended he had given up that dangerous thing called literature, were, in fact, filled with various writings he called scribblings.[12] While sequestered in his lair, where he scratched out fables and often unfinished stories and plays with his amateur's pen and scales on his amateur's violin, he kept the potentially competitive relations rich and humorous between the bourgeois household of *his* Augusta and the artist's

10. "Lo Sviluppo," *Opera,* 3:638; "Soggiorno londinese," *Opera,* 3:688.
11. Svevo to his wife, Livia Veneziani, June 6, 1900, *Opera,* 1:195.
12. "Pagine di diario e sparse," December 1902, *Opera,* 3:818.

study. Caricaturing himself as a bit of a businessman and a bit of an artist, he could become a quite a bit better amateur father and husband. This negotiation, practiced by Zeno as well, distinguishes him markedly from the great modern writers to whom he has so often been compared for their shared interest in Schopenhauer, Darwin, Nietzsche, and Freud, and their terminological conversion of "good" and "bad" into "sickness" and "health." Not for Svevo the radical rebellion of Kafka under a comparably defensive humor, though he must clearly have recognized, in a late discovery, a remarkable affinity between "The Judgment" and the section of his novel "The Death of My Father." In Kafka's stories, the rage and resentment of the artist clinging to his desk in his father's house are slyly relieved by an absurd and celibate humor that can avenge, only by self-annihilation, the bourgeois father's professional success in marriage and business. Zeno, whose humor helps him to survive and marry well, becomes with full irony, instead of a bug, or a superfluous man, the new "patriarch" of the family (IS, *Zeno,* 142). Nor would Svevo subscribe to the inevitability of a painful, death-intoxicated division projected by Thomas Mann between the worlds of art and business. A war even more severe in its satire between the claims of art and those of a social and sexual world is waged from the cork-lined study of Proust. Most readers would excuse Svevo from these over-extended comparisons, and Svevo himself, even if he might have known he served as a model for the endearingly defensive, marginal, international amateur Bloom, was content to distance his temperament from that of Joyce, a master of virtuosity, or from Proust, who "is so much finer than I . . . it's not possible that such a rude man as I could resemble the most perfect product of such a refined civilization." Svevo could not have served the Brecht who sarcastically protested Lukács's conservative standards of realist representation: "If Joyce had only set his monologue in a session with a psychoanalyst, everything would have been all right."[13]

He protects himself against their reputations by having us think of these masters as *professional* literary geniuses whose novels harbored many of the same themes he explored, and whose sophisticated resistance to the domesticated and casual negotiation of contested spheres and humors made Svevo seem a mere amateur. The posture of literary amateur, like that of musical, industrial, familial, political amateur, was an identification indispensable to the energy that might be choked off by humiliation or rejection. The humorous literary vengeance he takes on his friend Eduardo Weiss, the psychoanalyst, for his abrupt, professional response to a reading of *Confessions of Zeno*—"But this book has nothing, whatsoever, to do with

13. Svevo to Valerio Jahier, December 2, 1927, *Opera,* 1:857; "Scritti su Joyce," *Opera,* 3:729. Bertolt Brecht, "Against Lukács," 73.

psychoanalysis"—frees the novelist to his game. Fantasizing out of Einstein's theory of relativity, Svevo muses in an essay: "Suppose a man were constructed whose heart beat only once every ten minutes. That man would see the sun pass from one horizon to another with the rapidity of a firecracker." The daydreamer receives the same rebuff from Einstein that Svevo received from Weiss: "The idea is very nice, but it has nothing to do with my theory of relativity." A characteristic fable has changed resentment to the pleasure of a new fiction happy to go its own way without professional blessing, and equally happy to include us in the journey. We novelists falsify systems, admits Svevo, but only to humanize them.[14] *Confessions of Zeno,* only apparently a victim of arbitrary and abrupt narrative ordering, is symmetrically shaped by the amateur's conversation between all theories and their ironic and social qualifications in the body of Zeno.

Poor Dr. S., the consummate professional, always sure of dominating, is unaware of what the novel has done to him. Honoring the analyst's claim that his patient hated his father-in-law as a proxy father, Zeno must also mock the therapeutic air of omniscience that would emasculate the rich and delightful life we have seen spreading through the book:

> There are so many people who think it impossible to live in the world without a certain amount of affection; but I, according to him, was quite lost without a modicum of hatred. I wanted to marry one or other of his daughters, it did not matter which, because all I needed was to see their father in a position where I could reach him with my hatred. I did my best to dishonour the family I had married into, so far as it lay in my power; I was unfaithful to my wife, and, if I had been able, it was clear that I would have seduced Ada and Alberta. Of course I am not attempting to deny this, and it even made me laugh when the doctor, in saying it, put on an air of Christopher Columbus discovering America. All the same I think he must be the only person in the world who, hearing that I wanted to go to bed with two lovely women, must rack his brain to try and find a reason for it. (IS, *Zeno,* 376)

Even Dr. S.'s counterstroke, publishing at his own expense Zeno's confessions, is a move that must have afforded great amusement to Svevo, who regularly, befitting the amateur novelist, had to pay for the publication of his own novels. Svevo once fantasized a reaction from Freud: "Thank you for having introduced psychoanalysis into Italian culture"; and he would have envied Arthur Schnitzler for this actual testimonial from the father of psychoanalysis: "your determinism and your scepticism—what people call pessimism—your deep grasp of the truths of the unconscious and of the biological nature of man, the way you take to pieces the social conventions of our society, and the extent to which your thoughts are preoccupied with

14. "Soggiorno londinese," *Opera,* 3:686–87.

the polarity of love and death; all that moves me with an uncanny feeling of familiarity. So the impression has been borne in on me that you know through intuition—really from a delicate self-observation—everything that I have discovered in other people by laborious work. Indeed, I believe that fundamentally you are an explorer of the depths."[15] Yet he knew that such official, professional recognition was not good for his soul. Where Freud might make a theory out of his self-analysis, Svevo could only invent Zeno out of his and let Augusta's sister, Alberta, even while rejecting his marriage proposal, give him the response he desired: "Don't be offended, Zeno, for I should hate to hurt your feelings. I respect you very much. I think you're a very nice fellow, and you understand lots of things without having learnt them, whereas my professors only know what they have learnt" (IS, *Zeno,* 121).

An amateur like that can free Schopenhauer, Nietzsche, Darwin, Freud, felt everywhere in the novel, from their own systems. Players in a universe scored by many grammars and open to the speculations of psychoanalysis, the stock market, and Mother Nature, they cannot be professorial. Like Mother Nature, the novel has its own plan for its species: it pushes professionals from behind when they think they are being pulled from the front. This is the comic vengeance visited on Dr. S., on Olivi (the choice of Zeno's father to manage his son's money), on Guido (who is slated to be the sober professional patriarch of the family), on Dr. Coprosich (who reproaches the already guilt-ridden Zeno at the death of his father). Such a doctor would have simply diagnosed with precision Ada's disfigurement as Basedow's disease, an illness Svevo borrowed from one of Freud's dreams,[16] but Zeno, in the teeth of her former rejection of him as a suitor, transforms her malady into that great and humanizing bond that prevents anyone from being cut out of the herd, especially one who has been loved. Like Montaigne, Svevo will give us the best of the amateur's defenses against disappointment: he lets Zeno make of disease itself, instead of an isolating doom, a common metaphor for life:

all living beings are ranged along a certain line, at the end of which is Basedow's disease. All who are suffering from this disease use up their vital force recklessly in a mad vertiginous rhythm, the heart beating without control. At the other end of the line are those wretched beings, shriveled up by native avarice, and doomed to die from a disease that looks like exhaustion and is really cowardice. The happy mean between these two maladies is to be found in the middle of the line, and is called health, though it is really only a suspension of movement. Between the center and Basedow's end are to be found all those

15. Svevo, "Profilo autobiografica," *Opera,* 3:807; Ernest Jones, *Life and Work of Sigmund Freud,* 3:443–44.

16. Freud, "Interpretation of Dreams," *Works,* 4:269.

whose life is consumed in desire, ambition, pleasure, or even work; toward the opposite end those who merely sprinkle crumbs on the plate of life and eke out a long, miserable existence that can only be a burden to society. (IS, *Zeno,* 287)

Zeno's version of life as purgatory manages to give both a moral and a psychological superiority to Ada's fellow Basedowans. If, like all great amateurs, we have to keep moving in life to avoid becoming poisoned, or to profit from life's antidotes, we are not in diaspora, but in family. This includes, of course, even those like Dr. S. purveying cures. Psychoanalysis, which Zeno at one time demotes to the spiritualism practiced by Guido, will not save us from professional pretensions and destructions. Still, in an over-generous ascription of his metaphor to the doctor, Zeno is willing not to blame him "for regarding life itself as a manifestation of a disease," even if he is dangerously mistaken to think it can be cured (IS, *Zeno,* 397). Only the patient, hero of the novel, could see widely enough and generously enough to democratize disease.

He sees around all those aficionados of war, of systems, of professions, who would have their final solutions, and expands our scene into the soothing atmosphere of lyric Nature, which eases moral dilemmas without canceling them, calms the passion for cure without curing it. In one of the finest of these scenes that frame the bourgeois parlor with sentient sea and stars, humbling such ultimates as resolutions to stop smoking, Zeno has just been wounded by the violin virtuosity of Guido, continuous with his victorious courtship of Ada. The victor insists on tempering the slur of "amateur" flung at him by his future brother-in-law —"he did not choose to rank as a professional" (IS, *Zeno,* 129)—leaving that felicitous state intact for Zeno. Guido contaminates even his victory in love by pontificating on the incapacities for genius and goodness in women, cribbed from Otto Weininger's misogynistic theories. Zeno, needing both to feel resentment and to mediate it socially, fancies Guido might be offering him a consolation prize as the spoils of defeat in love; more likely the selfish, humorless, and insensitive Guido is justifying, by anticipation, his own future betrayals and failures as a husband. Viewing him perched precariously on a wall, Zeno disarms his guilt-evoking urge to push him off, revamping his game of preventing disaster by wishing it; he simulates a loud moan of pain to summon Guido down from danger. It is a gesture that, in its capacity to clear away rivalry, hostility, and theory itself, seems "important enough to be compared to the great moon climbing up the sky and sweeping it clean" (IS, *Zeno,* 114–16, 131).

In a later pastoral walk, with Guido now desperate, Zeno will deflect his brother-in-law's debilitating self-pity, climaxing in the capitulating cliché "Life is hard and unjust," by his instinctively sane and seminal adage,

"Life is neither good nor bad; it is original." Immediately, the space opens up beyond the physician's clinical study and prepares us for the final prophecy of the novel: "When I thought it over I felt as if I had said something rather important. Looking at it like that I felt as if I were seeing life for the first time, with all its gaseous, liquid, and solid bodies. If I had talked about it to someone who was strange to it, and therefore deprived of an ordinary common sense, he would have remained gasping at the thought of the huge, purposeless structure. He would have asked: "But how could you endure it?" And if he had inquired about everything in detail, from the heavenly bodies hung up in the sky which can be seen but not touched, to the mystery that surrounds death, he would certainly have exclaimed: 'Very original!'" (IS, *Zeno,* 299). Zeno's attraction to this kind of perspective gives him a means of soothing his bourgeois soul, wracked with anxiety and guilt, because, once again, personal miseries have been democratized. Dr. S. might have suspected Zeno of only an escapist displacement in making originality an adequate morality, but because he is blocked out from the creativity of this view, he is rendered oblivious to the power of a lyrical and neutral world to frighten and startle us out of self-pitying psychological impasses. The kind of analysis and self-analysis practiced by Zeno, invariably the prelude to an explosively generous social scene, gravitates toward the edges of planetary space, not only for escape but for therapeutic relief from an incessant passion for innocence. If Svevo had known the Freud who begged the physician not to be a fanatic about health, we might never have had the pleasure of meeting Dr. S.

What allows Zeno to spread out in the multilayered atmosphere of the amateur's novel that holds Dr. S.'s vengeance up to laughter is the fullness of the identification between the temperaments of Zeno and of his author. Henry James chose the term *saturation* to describe the sense of a sumptuous entry into characters, to free them from mere type, by novelists like Balzac, and made it his highest moral as well as aesthetic category, like Montaigne's "consubstantiality" between body and book, because he believed: "When saturation fails no other presence really avails; as when, on the other hand, it operates, no failure of method fatally interferes." Montale, echoing many others who met Svevo, describes the thoroughness of his saturation in his work: "I have met many famous writers, both foreign and Italian, and almost always, even when I have not been disappointed, I have had to distinguish between the man and the writer: in all these cases, the scale went down on one side or the other but at any rate the scale dipped. Not in the case of Svevo: in him one felt a presence that was all of a piece."[17] Svevo humors his shortcomings by making the amateurism of

17. HJ, "Balz," *Crit,* 2:131; Montale, *Lettere,* 125, 152.

Zeno a caricatured version of his own favored posture. Through his felici-
tously accidental courtship, through adultery, Zeno could be even more
amateur a husband than his author; through his fickle enrollments at the
university, culminating in idleness, more of an amateur careerist; through
his written confessions, more of an amateur writer; even more of an amateur of social thought than Svevo (who could waggishly swear to his future
wife that he would love her only as much as the fin de siècle allowed him)[18]
through his amusing fancy of using historical excuses for personal failings:
"As I hurried home I was even bold enough to begin attacking our social
system, as if that were responsible for my shortcomings" (IS, *Zeno*, 194).
And because Zeno expands his creator's cigarette smoking to guilts and
rebellions associated with a father and mistress, he becomes, even more
than Svevo, an amateur of resolve. To rationalize the modesty of his violin
playing, Svevo has Zeno theorize that because he feels music so deeply,
he is doomed to be unable to give others the pleasure of a professional per-
formance (IS, *Zeno*, 103). Zeno embroiders his author's willingness, much
discussed by critics, to be an amateur Jew. Like him, Zeno allows himself to
be lured by love and marriage into an awkward cooperation with his wife's
religion: "Augusta's religion did not take time to acquire or put into practice. You bowed your knee and returned to ordinary life again immediately!
That was all. Religion for me was a very different thing. If I had only believed, nothing else in the world would have mattered to me" (IS, *Zeno*,
152). But with the certainty of faith, we would have a professional Zeno,
who, appropriating a version of Proust's design, would obstruct the Svevian continuity between book and writer.

The sources of Zeno's gay and sociable wisdom, like those of Montaigne's,
are constant and moving conversations with personal sickness and the
sickness of systematic philosophy. He has been called, for that, an heir of
the underground man. But, cut off from the active love of Christianity that
would have socialized him, Dostoyevsky's underground man, by his author's own admission, was a central *professional* modern type.[19] The saturation Dostoyevsky allowed himself with his underground man—which
gave life to his acute critical animus directed against social utopians, ratio-
nal egoists, utilitarians, the Mills, Darwins, Strausses—his antihero thank-
lessly turned into a sour game of self-hate and justification that made of all
potential engagement an opportunity for taking or giving offense, humiliation and domination, condescension and scorn. Like Dr. S., the underground man has tendentious wit, but not the humor that Freud insisted

18. "Diario della fidanzata," January 26, 1896, *Opera*, 3:780.
19. See Dostoyevsky's footnote on the first page of *Notes from Underground*, 3. Henceforth cited in the text as FD, *Notes*.

helps us to evade the *compulsion* to suffer, and that Svevo insisted helps us
to transcend the compulsion to fight: "When the World War broke out, I
was grieved over every defeat because I certainly had no need of a war
to free me from hate."[20] The painful longing for cures, for innocence, for
health, hyperconsciously acknowledged by the underground man and Zeno,
can only by an infectious humor be shared with the so-called normal man,
largely unaware even of the problem. While the underground man sports
his sickness as a divisive distinction, a sign of professional superiority in
the art of suffering, Zeno amateurizes his by improvisations and adages
that overcome envy or the pride of privilege. He exhibits with Dostoyevsky's
antihero the obsession to talk as a compensation for an inability to act,
but while the underground man turns his speech to flagellation and self-
flagellation, Zeno turns his to the action of converting self-pity, envy, and
guilt into occasions for communal laughter. When Dostoyevsky's Liza is
courted by the underground man in patronizing and sentimental rhetoric,
a self-acknowledged symptom of his inability to live and love, she explodes
the tactic in his face: "Why, you talk just like a book" (FD, *Notes,* 86).
Meanwhile, Zeno has his books talk like *him:* "Perhaps this time I was
impelled by a strong desire to get into touch with Augusta and become
perfectly healthy like her. Going to mass with her was not enough; I must
get there in other ways, such as reading Renan and Strauss, the first with
great enjoyment, the second as punishment. I only mention it here to show
how great was my desire to come nearer to Augusta" (IS, *Zeno,* 152). The
European intellectual mentors Zeno has studied are not trounced for the
sake of trashing the normal active life that is rejecting him. And, in a fine
variation of Liza's rebuke, he decides not to disabuse Guido of his assumption that he read somewhere his adage on life's originality so as not to
distract the delight that diverts Guido's self-pity. Because he *is* a modern
hero, Zeno harbors, with the underground man, the habits of fetishistic
hyperconsciousness, divided internally between slave and master, an anxious sensation of conflicting moods and motives, a compulsion to rationalize and lie, to correct those lies in bad faith, a vulnerability to competition,
envy, self-pity, hypochondria. And it is important to spot the psychological
diseases of modern man in Zeno, of modern novelists in Svevo. But even as
we compare, it is more important to witness how consistently Svevo and his
Zeno refuse to profit from disease at the expense of a society they both love.
The underground man hangs on for dear life to his historical and class
displacements of blame, continually subjecting us to the plaints of an educated man of the nineteenth century suffering from the "toothache of progress and European civilization" (FD, *Notes,* 13). Zeno, like Svevo, smiles at

20. "Pagine di diario," *Opera,* 3:828.

the temptation to hide behind historical fin-de-siècle fate. While the underground man's cacophonous cadenzas punish, divorce, divide, and pretend to want no audience, Zeno's improvisations always solicit the bourgeois laughter that changes funerals to weddings. They neutralize fantasies of vengeance that possess the underground man, pale ghosts of direct Balzacian action no longer possible.

Because amateurism is a dedicated enemy of applied purity, perfection, and cures, its tolerance of our longing for them makes it an honest and humane therapist. The underground man, justifying his own case by diagnosing the century, is suspicious of his right to use "all of us" (FD, Notes, 114–15). But when Zeno romances his oedipal complex into his conversations with the world, assumes the mantle of Basedow's disease, he is denying to the underground man the special pleading of his proud, transvaluating opening declaration—"I am a sick man"—and forging an authority for his own climactic "we." While Dostoyevsky's professional bug uses his sickness to become a superman of analytic scorn, Zeno uses his to become a democratic agent of a common health through judicious, sophistical wit: if we have never been cured, could we have had a disease (IS, Zeno, 367)? Svevo himself, in a letter of 1927 in which he calls Freud more valuable for literature than for therapy, breaks us out of the quarantine imposed by logical systems by asking, "Why should we wish to cure our sickness? Ought we to take away from humanity what is best about it?"[21]

Professional theorists and specialists, like Nietzsche's priestly caste, become more and more destructive as they make us weaker and weaker on the Darwinian scale. The prophetic end of the novel returns us to Schopenhauer's vision of a universe free of applied cures, an earth relieved of its human parasites, this time by the bombs of technocrats relieved of temperament. Though it is a picture not uncommon in the literature of the late nineteenth and early twentieth century, it seems prescient to citizens of the atomic age. Its most important function might be to remind us that we need to build societies capable of laughing at our common diseases and defects, deployed in various intensities and measures along Basedow's line, to keep ourselves from suffocating on our professionalisms. Zeno's financial killing in wartime might attract the charge of immorality, but it succeeds in humbling the transvaluating call of political patriots and supermen to the final great cure: war. Because Zeno must go on being both good-bad and original, binding, like the Italian title word coscienza, conscience and consciousness, he carries Svevo's deepest wisdom. He beckons all of us to live in a world where everything, as Montale said of him, is Svevian from head

21. Svevo to Valerio Jahier, December 10, 1927, Opera, 1:857.

to toe.[22] It takes a novel this original, touching, and amusing to imagine a time when we will not need all its psychological twists and turns, its tortuous negotiations, to educate and console us. Svevo can envision, in one of his scribblings, a utopian society weaned from the comforts of literature and content with the luxury of laughter: "Perhaps when we finally are released from space and time we will know each other so intimately that we will have a direct path to sincerity. We will speak with familiarity to each other and laugh at each other in turn, as we deserve. Literature, which now, unfortunately, is so intimate a part of our soul, will finally perish and we will see each other immediately and deeply."[23] But the prospect of such perfection, like any perfection, to a novelist delighting in the mysteries of the human personality provokes Svevo's immediate deflation: "gruesome prospect." He returns us to the Svevian world of the novel where we make our moral life by laughing at ourselves and each other, even when, like Zeno's stock-market luck, it may be more than we deserve.

22. Montale, *Lettere,* February 21, 1946, 131–32.
23. "Pagine sparse," *Opera,* 3:829.

BIBLIOGRAPHY

Arnold, Matthew. *Complete Prose Works.* 11 vols. Edited by R. H. Super. Ann Arbor: University of Michigan Press, 1960–1978.

Auerbach, Erich. *Mimesis: The Representation of Reality in Western Literature.* Translated by Willard Trask. Garden City: Doubleday, 1957.

Bakhtin, M. M. *The Dialogic Imagination: Four Essays.* Edited by Michael Holquist. Translated by Caryl Emerson and Michael Holquist. Austin: University of Texas Press, 1981.

———. *Problems of Dostoevsky's Poetics.* Edited and translated by Caryl Emerson. Minneapolis: University of Minnesota Press, 1984.

Balzac, Honoré de. *Correspondance de Balzac.* 5 vols. Edited by Roger Pierrot. Paris: Garnier, 1960–1969.

———. *Cousin Bette.* Translated by Marion Ayton Crawford. Baltimore: Penguin, 1965.

———. *Cousin Pons.* Translated by Herbert J. Hunt. Baltimore: Penguin, 1968.

———. *Lost Illusions.* Translated by Robert Baldick. Harmondsworth: Penguin, 1971.

———. *Oeuvres de Honoré de Balzac.* 24 vols. Paris: Calmann Levy, 1875–1892.

Barthes, Roland. *Mythologies.* Translated by Annette Lavers. New York: Hill and Wang, 1972.

Bennett, Arnold. *Books and Persons: Being Comments on a Past Epoch, 1908–1911.* New York: George H. Doran, 1917.

Bernheimer, Charles. *Flaubert and Kafka: Studies in Psychopoetic Structure.* New Haven: Yale University Press, 1982.

Brecht, Bertolt. "Against Lukács." Translated by Stuart Hood. In *Aesthetics and Politics: Ernst Bloch, Georg Lukács, Bertolt Brecht, Walter Benjamin, Theodor Adorno.* London: NLB, 1977.

Brooks, Peter. *Body Work: Objects of Desire in Modern Narrative.* Cambridge: Harvard University Press, 1993.

————. *The Melodramatic Imagination: Balzac, Henry James, Melodrama, and the Mode of Excess*. New York: Columbia University Press, 1985.

Burnshaw, Stanley. *Robert Frost Himself.* New York: George Braziller, 1986.

Butor, Michel. *Improvisations sur Flaubert*. Paris: Le Sphinx, 1984.

Conrad, Joseph. *Joseph Conrad on Fiction*. Edited by Walter F. Wright. Lincoln: University of Nebraska Press, 1967.

————. *Lord Jim*. Edited by Thomas Moser. New York: W. W. Norton, 1968.

————. *The Mirror of the Sea*. In *"The Mirror of the Sea" and "A Personal Record,"* edited by Morton Dauwen Zabel. Garden City: Doubleday, 1960.

————. *Nigger of the "Narcissus."* Edited by Robert Kimbrough. New York: W. W. Norton, 1979.

————. *A Personal Record: Some Reminiscences*. In *"The Mirror of the Sea" and "A Personal Record,"* edited by Morton Dauwen Zabel. Garden City: Doubleday, 1960.

Dickens, Charles. *Hard Times*. Harmondsworth: Penguin, 1971.

Diderot, Denis. *"Rameau's Nephew" and "d'Alembert's Dream."* Translated by Leonard Tancock. Harmondsworth: Penguin, 1966.

Dostoyevsky, Fyodor. *Notes from Underground*. In *"Notes from Underground" with "The Grand Inquisitor,"* translated and edited by Ralph A. Matlaw. New York: E. P. Dutton, 1960.

du Bos, Charles. *Approximations*. Paris: Fayard, 1965.

Edel, Leon. *The Life of Henry James*. 5 vols. New York: Avon Books, 1953.

Emerson, Ralph Waldo. *Selected Essays of Ralph Waldo Emerson*. Edited by Larzer Ziff. Harmondsworth: Penguin, 1982.

————. *Selections from Ralph Waldo Emerson*. Edited by Stephen E. Whicher. Boston: Houghton Mifflin, 1970.

Flaubert, Gustave. *The Letters of Gustave Flaubert, 1857–1880*. Translated and edited by Francis Steegmuller. Cambridge: Harvard University Press, 1982.

————. *Madame Bovary*. Translated by Alan Russell. Harmondsworth: Penguin, 1950.

————. *Selected Letters of Gustave Flaubert*. Translated and edited by Francis Steegmuller. New York: Farrar, Straus and Cudahy, 1953.

————. *Sentimental Education*. Translated by Robert Baldick. Baltimore: Penguin, 1964.

Freud, Sigmund. *The Standard Edition of Complete Psychological Works of Sigmund Freud*. 24 vols. Translated by James Strachey and Anna Freud. London: Hogarth Press, 1953–1974.

Frost, Robert. *The Poetry of Robert Frost: Collected Poems*. Edited by Edward Connery Lathem. New York: Henry Holt, 1979.

————. "Robert Frost: The Art of Poetry, II." Interview by Richard Poirier. *Paris Review* 24 (summer–fall 1960): 88–120.

————. *Robert Frost: Poetry and Prose.* Edited by Edward Connery Lathem and Lawrance Thompson. New York: Holt, Rinehart and Winston, 1972.

————. *Robert Frost on Writing.* Introduced and edited by Elaine Barry. New Brunswick: Rutgers University Press, 1973.

————. *Selected Letters of Robert Frost.* Edited by Lawrance Thompson. New York: Holt, Rinehart and Winston, 1964.

Fussell, Edwin Sill. *The French Side of Henry James.* New York: Columbia University Press, 1990.

The Goncourt Journals, 1851–1876. Translated and edited by Lewis Galantiere. Garden City: Doubleday, 1958.

Grover, Philip. *Henry James and the French Novel.* London: Paul Elek, 1973.

Hardy, Thomas. *The Life and Work of Thomas Hardy.* Edited by Michael Millgate. Athens: University of Georgia Press, 1985.

Hocks, Richard A. *Henry James and Pragmatist Thought: A Study in the Relationship between the Philosophy of William James and the Literary Art of Henry James.* Chapel Hill: University of North Carolina Press, 1974.

James, Henry. *Literary Criticism.* Vol. 1, *Essays on Literature; American Writers; English Writers.* Vol. 2, *French Writers; Other European Writers; The Prefaces to the New York Edition.* Edited by Leon Edel, with the assistance of Mark Wilson. New York: Library of America, 1984.

————. *The Notebooks of Henry James.* Edited by F. O. Matthiessen and Kenneth B. Murdock. New York: George Braziller, 1955.

————. *The Portrait of a Lady.* Harmondsworth: Penguin, 1986.

————. *The Scenic Art: Notes on Acting and the Drama, 1872–1901.* Edited by Allan Wade. New Brunswick: Rutgers University Press, 1948.

————. *Henry James: Selected Letters.* Edited by Leon Edel. Cambridge: Harvard University Press, 1987.

————. *The Wings of the Dove.* Harmondsworth: Penguin, 1965.

James, Henry, Sr. *The Literary Remains of the Late Henry James.* Introduced and edited by William James. Boston: Houghton Mifflin, 1897.

James, William. *Essays in Radical Empiricism.* Edited by Fredson Bowers and Ignas K. Skrupskelis. Cambridge: Harvard University Press, 1976.

————. *The Meaning of Truth.* In *"Pragmatism" and "The Meaning of Truth,"* edited by Fredson Bowers and Ignas K. Skrupskelis. Cambridge: Harvard University Press, 1978.

————. *A Pluralistic Universe.* Edited by Fredson Bowers and Ignas K. Skrupskelis. Cambridge: Harvard University Press, 1977.

————. *Pragmatism.* In *"Pragmatism" and "The Meaning of Truth,"* edited by Fredson Bowers and Ignas K. Skrupskelis. Cambridge: Harvard University Press, 1978.

118

BIBLIOGRAPHY

————. *The Selected Letters of William James.* Introduced and edited by Elizabeth Hardwick. Boston: Godine, 1980.

————. *Some Problems of Philosophy.* Edited by Frederick H. Burkhardt, Fredson Bowers, and Ignas K. Skrupskelis. Cambridge: Harvard University Press, 1979.

————. *The Varieties of Religious Experience.* Edited by Martin E. Marty. Harmondsworth: Penguin, 1982.

————. *The Will to Believe.* In *"The Will to Believe" and Other Essays in Popular Philosophy,* edited by Frederick H. Burkhardt, Fredson Bowers, and Ignas K. Skrupskelis. Cambridge: Harvard University Press, 1979.

————. *The Writings of William James.* Introduced and Edited by John J. McDermott. New York: Random House, 1967.

Jones, Ernest. *Life and Work of Sigmund Freud.* 3 vols. New York: Basic Books, 1953.

Jones, Vivien. *Henry James the Critic.* New York: St. Martin's Press, 1985.

Joyce, James. *Ulysses.* Edited by Hans Walter Gabler with Wolfhard Steppe and Claus Melchior. New York: Random House, 1986.

Kernan, Alvin. *Samuel Johnson and the Impact of Print.* Princeton: Princeton University Press, 1987.

Lawrence, D. H. *Phoenix: The Posthumous Papers.* Edited by Edward D. McDonald. Harmondsworth: Penguin, 1978.

————. *Psychoanalysis and the Unconscious.* In *"Psychoanalysis and the Unconscious" with "Fantasia of the Unconscious."* Introduced and edited by Philip Rieff. New York: Viking Press, 1960.

————. *The Selected Letters of D. H. Lawrence.* Edited by Diana Trilling. New York: Farrar, Straus and Cudahy, 1958.

Leavis, F. R. *The Great Tradition.* Garden City: Doubleday, 1954.

Lebowitz, Naomi. *Ibsen and the Great World.* Baton Rouge: Louisiana State University Press, 1990.

Lentricchia, Frank. *Ariel and the Police: Michel Foucault, William James, Wallace Stevens.* Madison: University of Wisconsin Press, 1988.

————. *Robert Frost: Modern Poetics and the Landscape of Self.* Durham: Duke University Press, 1975.

Levin, Harry. *The Gates of Horn: A Study of Five French Realists.* New York: Oxford University Press, 1963.

Martin, Terence. "The Negative Structure of American Literature." *American Literature* 57 (March 1985): 1–22.

Mauriac, François. *Men I Hold Great.* Translated by Elsie Pell. New York: Philosophical Library, 1951.

Montaigne, Michel de. *The Complete Essays of Montaigne.* 3 vols. in 1. Translated and edited by Donald M. Frame. Stanford: Stanford University Press, 1958.

Montale, Eugenio. *Lettere Italo Svevo: con gli scritti di Montale su Svevo.* Bari: De Donato, 1966.

Murdoch, Iris. *Metaphysics as a Guide to Morals.* New York: Viking Press, 1992.

Myers, Gerald E. *William James: His Life and Thought.* New Haven: Yale University Press, 1986.

Newton, Ruth, and Naomi Lebowitz. *Dickens, Manzoni, Zola, and James: The Impossible Romance.* Columbia: University of Missouri Press, 1990.

Nietzsche, Friedrich. *Basic Writings of Nietzsche.* Translated and edited by Walter Kaufmann. New York: Modern Library, 1968.

―――. *Beyond Good and Evil.* Translated and edited by Walter Kaufmann. New York: Random House, 1966.

―――. *The Genealogy of Morals.* In *"The Birth of Tragedy" and "The Genealogy of Morals,"* translated by Francis Golffing. Garden City: Doubleday, 1956.

―――. *The Gay Science.* Translated and edited by Walter Kaufmann. New York: Random House, 1974.

―――. "Expeditions of an Untimely Man." In *"Twilight of the Idols" and "The Anti-Christ,"* translated by R. J. Hollingdale. Harmondsworth: Penguin, 1968.

Peterson, Margaret. *Wallace Stevens and the Idealist Tradition.* Ann Arbor: UMI Research Press, 1983.

Pirandello, Luigi. *Opere.* 6 vols. Edited by Manlio Lo Vecchio-Musti. Milan: Mondadori, 1964–1965.

Poirier, Richard. *Poetry and Pragmatism.* Cambridge: Harvard University Press, 1992.

―――. *The Renewal of Literature: Emersonian Reflections.* New Haven: Yale University Press, 1977.

―――. *Robert Frost: The Work of Knowing.* New York: Oxford University Press, 1977.

Posnock, Ross. *The Trial of Curiosity: Henry James, William James, and the Challenge of Modernity.* New York: Oxford University Press, 1991.

Proust, Marcel. *Letters of Marcel Proust.* Translated by Mina Curtiss. New York: Random House, 1949.

―――. *Marcel Proust on Art and Literature, 1896–1919.* Translated by Sylvia Townsend Warner. New York: Meridian, 1958.

―――. *Remembrance of Things Past.* 3 vols. Translated by C. K. Scott Moncrieff and Terence Kilmartin. New York: Random House, 1981.

Richard, Jean-Pierre. "The Creation of Form in Flaubert," translated by Raymond Giraud. In *Flaubert: A Collection of Essays,* edited by Raymond Giraud. Englewood Cliffs: Prentice-Hall, 1964.

Robbe-Grillet, Alain. *For a New Novel: Essays on Fiction.* Translated by Richard Howard. New York: Grove Press, 1965.

Rorty, Richard. *Contingency, Irony, and Solidarity.* Cambridge: Cambridge University Press, 1989.

————. *Philosophy and the Mirror of Nature.* Princeton: Princeton University Press, 1979.

Rousseau, Jean-Jacques. *The Confessions.* Translated by J. M. Cohen. Baltimore: Penguin, 1963.

————. "A Discourse on the Moral Effects of the Arts and Sciences." In *"The Social Contract" and "Discourses,"* translated by G. D. H. Cole and revised by J. H. Brumfitt and John C. Hall, 2–26. London: Everyman's Library, 1973.

————. *La Nouvelle Héloise: Julie, or the New Eloise.* Translated and abridged by Judith H. McDowell. University Park: Pennsylvania State University Press, 1968.

————. *Politics and the Arts: Letter to M. D'Alembert on the Theatre.* Translated by Allan Bloom. Glencoe, Ill.: Free Press, 1960.

————. *The Reveries of the Solitary Walker.* Translated and edited by Charles E. Butterworth. New York: New York University Press, 1979.

Ruland, Richard, ed. *A Storied Land: Theories of American Literature.* 2 vols. New York: E. P. Dutton, 1976.

Ruskin, John. *Modern Painters.* 5 vols. London: J. M. Dent & Co., 1906.

————. *The Seven Lamps of Architecture.* New York: Dover, 1989.

Sainte-Beuve, Charles A. *Literary Criticism of Sainte-Beuve.* Translated and edited by Emerson R. Marks. Lincoln: University of Nebraska Press, 1971.

Santayana, George. "Apologia Pro Mente Sua." In *The Philosophy of George Santayana,* edited by Paul Arthur Schilpp. New York: Tudor Publishing Co., 1951.

————. *Character and Opinion in the United States.* Garden City: Doubleday, 1954.

————. *Interpretations of Poetry and Religion.* Edited by William G. Holzberger and Herman J. Saatkamp, Jr. Cambridge: MIT Press, 1990.

————. *Reason in Art.* New York: Collier, 1962.

————. *Reason in Common Sense.* New York: Collier, 1962.

————. *Reason in Religion.* New York: Dover, 1982.

————. *The Philosophy of Santayana.* Introduced and edited by Irwin Edman. New York: Random House, 1936.

————. *Three Philosophical Poets: Lucretius, Dante, Goethe.* Garden City: Doubleday, 1938.

————. *Winds of Doctrine.* In *"Winds of Doctrine" with "Platonism and the Spiritual Life."* New York: Harper and Brothers, 1957.

Sartre, Jean-Paul. *Literary Essays.* Translated by Annette Michelson. New York: Philosophical Library, 1957.

————. *Nausea.* Translated by Lloyd Alexander. New York: New Directions, 1964.

Shklar, Judith. *Ordinary Vices.* Cambridge: Harvard University Press, 1984.

Solaria 4:3–4 (March–April 1929). A special issue on Svevo, "Omaggio a Italo Svevo," including articles by G. B. Angioletti and Piero Gadda.

Spacks, Patricia Meyer. *Gossip.* New York: Knopf, 1985.

Stendhal. *Red and Black.* Translated by Robert M. Adams. New York: W. W. Norton, 1969.

Stevens, Wallace. *The Collected Poems.* New York: Random House, 1954.

————. *The Letters of Wallace Stevens.* Edited by Holly Stevens. New York: Knopf, 1966.

————. *The Necessary Angel: Essays on Reality and the Imagination.* New York: Random House, 1965.

————. *Opus Posthumous: Poems, Plays, Prose.* Edited by Milton J. Bates. New York: Random House, 1965.

Stowe, William W. *Balzac, James, and the Realistic Novel.* Princeton: Princeton University Press, 1983.

Svevo, Italo. *Confessions of Zeno.* Translated by Beryl de Zoete. New York: Random House, 1961.

————. *Opera omnia.* 3 vols. Edited by Bruno Maier. Milan: dall 'Oglio, 1966.

Taine, Hippolyte. *Balzac: A Critical Study.* Translated by Lorenzo O'Rourke. New York: Haskell House, 1973.

————. *The History of English Literature.* 4 vols. Translated by H. Van Laun. Philadelphia: David McKay, 1890.

Tanner, Tony. *Adultery in the Novel: Contract and Transgression.* Baltimore: Johns Hopkins University Press, 1979.

Tintner, Adeline R. *The Book World of Henry James.* Ann Arbor: UMI Research Press, 1987.

————. *The Cosmopolitan World of Henry James: An Intertextual Study.* Baton Rouge: Louisiana State University Press, 1991.

Vendler, Helen. *Words Chosen Out of Desire.* Cambridge: Harvard University Press, 1986.

Woolf, Virginia. *The Common Reader.* 2 vols. in 1. New York: Harcourt, Brace, 1932.

————. *The Essays of Virginia Woolf.* 3 vols. Edited by Andrew McNeillie. New York: Harcourt Brace Jovanovich, 1988.

————. *A Room of One's Own.* New York: Harcourt Brace Jovanovich, 1989.

————. *Three Guineas.* New York: Harcourt Brace Jovanovich, 1966.

————. *To the Lighthouse.* New York: Harcourt Brace Jovanovich, 1989.

INDEX